T0099102

INVINCIBLE SUMMER

INVINCIBLE SUMMER

Traveling America in Search
of Yesterday's Baseball Greats

Dave D'Antonio

Diamond Communications, Inc.
South Bend, Indiana
1997

INVINCIBLE SUMMER

Copyright ©1997 by Dave D'Antonio

All rights reserved. No part of this book may be used or reproduced in any manner whatsoever without the written permission of the publisher.

10 9 8 7 6 5 4 3 2 1

Manufactured in the United States of America

Diamond Communications, Inc.
Post Office Box 88
South Bend, Indiana 46624-0088
Editorial: (219) 299-9278
Orders Only: 1-800-480-3717
Fax: (219) 299-9296

Library of Congress Cataloging-in-Publication Data

D'Antonio, Dave, 1960-
    Invincible summer : traveling America in search of
yesterday's baseball greats / Dave D'Antonio.
        p.   cm.
    ISBN 1-888698-08-X
    1. Baseball--United States--History.   2. United
States--Description and travel--Anecdotes.   3. Sepul-
chral monuments--United States--Anecdotes.   I. Title.
GV863.A1D36   1997   97-9838
                                                  CIP

THE LINEUP

ACKNOWLEDGMENTS

No journey taken alone, across the nation or even across the street, is truly solitary. Others have gone before, and go with, to either shape the traveler or to shape the route. My route and my journey were shaped by dozens of people.

Staci Frenes and Anita Schriver, my partners in teaching and laughing at Bancroft Middle School, were a constant help during the weeks preceding the trip. I am grateful to my principal, Dennis Berger, for letting me miss parts of two school years. He coached former Cy Young Award winner Mark Davis in high school, so this was perhaps his second major contribution to baseball. Sylvia Colt was a huge help with her computer expertise.

The road was made much easier by friends and acquaintances and, in some cases, strangers who opened their homes and refrigerators to an often weary traveler. The lineup is long but important. Thanks go to Beth and Chris Hauso in Redlands, California; Beth Clark and Kevin Kennedy in Grand Junction, Colorado; Roger and Hazel Parsell in Denver; Flossie Jacobson in St. Paul, Nebraska; David and Ann Nelson in Kansas City, Missouri; Mildred Miller in Quincy, Illinois; Steve Barrett in Columbia, Missouri; John Pleasant in Oklahoma City; Mary Catherine and Jim Monroe in Arlington, Texas; David and Marvela Paschall in Austin, Texas; Tim and Theresa Dowling in New Orleans; Steve Peterson in Atlanta; Peter and Robin Reibold in Columbia, South Carolina; Eric and Kerri Dvorak in Waxhaw, North Carolina; David Sahr and Lori Milstein in Washington, D.C.; Ben Leotta in Syracuse, New York; Stephen and Lenore Waldman in Sayville, New York; Alicia Alfaro in Flint, Michigan; Elin Schriver in Evanston, Illinois; Cary Sfikas in Minneapolis; Scott Gray in Cedar Falls, Iowa; Jim and Penny Fahey in Olympia, Washington; Jordona Elderts in Oakland, California; Dean and Claire Koenig and Mary and Ron Rodriguez, both in San Leandro, California; David and Yolanda Williams in Torrance, California; Angela Rocco in San Jose, California; and Judith Boyle in Fremont, California. Dozens of Holiday Inns across the country must also be acknowledged for the free use of their parking lots and facilities, particularly their bathrooms and hot tubs. I'm sorry I didn't think to write down their locations so I could thank them personally.

I am grateful to Nikki Frediani, a former student, whose going away gift of a blank notebook is now filled with drawings of the Hall of Famers' graves, and to Sid Schoenfeld for research help. Thanks also go to Chris Rogers, who is president of the Lefty O'Doul Chapter of the Society for American Baseball Research, for providing contacts and speaking opportunities.

Jill and Jim Langford at Diamond Communications will always have my appreciation for believing in this project. Thanks for taking a chance. Thanks also to Juanita Dix for her text and cover designs, and to Shari Hill for patiently answering scores of questions.

Much of the book was written at the home of Reed Parsell, who also lent me his tent, stove, and bike rack for the trip. These are small items compared to the gifts he has provided since our second day of college:

laughs, stories, competition, and countless talks on baseball and women.

Beth Clark has already been mentioned, but to not comment further would be akin to a baseball history book having only a solitary reference of Babe Ruth. Her belief and encouragement were more constant than the greatest of consecutive games streaks. I am forever grateful.

I am thankful for my family and am fortunate to be a part of it. My parents, Rosemary Brown and Harvey Lohmeyer, have supported me in all my endeavors, even the strange ones. I must mention my siblings because, well, because they're my siblings: Marisa, Ken, Nick, and Joseph. Special thanks to Joseph whose 800 number gave me access to home from any number of roadside phones when times were lonely.

Finally, I am thankful for and blessed by Ann Murray. Her smile and words and support make every season, every moment, not just memorable but wondrous.

To Mom and Dad.

And to the players who
gave me dreams as a child and
memories as an adult.

INTRODUCTION

Dan Brouthers is buried in a graveyard behind St. Mary's Catholic Church in Wappingers Falls, New York. A funeral was scheduled to begin soon after I arrived on a humid Tuesday morning in late July. I asked a priest why so many older churches doubled as burial grounds. They served as a messenger, he said. Marble and granite markers reminded the faithful that death is not the end of life but an extension.

Cemeteries have always interested me. My aunt and uncle lived across from a large cemetery in my hometown of Santa Clara, California. I visited them periodically, and from their porch looked through a fence to see a world I knew nothing about. Perhaps because of those moments of childhood gazing cemeteries never frightened me. I felt their peace and silence and respected their members. They were natural places. Good places. I felt comfortable there, as I did beside my uncle.

He was soft-spoken and gentle, qualities which made me wonder how he survived mining coal in the company town of Madrid, New Mexico. My uncle loved baseball. He adored the game and its players. His greeting was as constant as his warmth. In a voice that always sounded hoarse, he'd ask, "What about the Giants?" It wouldn't matter if they were the Giants of Willie Mays or Willie Montanez, of Bobby Bonds or Bob Barton.

In 1974 we attended our first game together. Strangely, it was an A's game. My uncle sat to my right, a blanket covering his legs and lap. Sal Bando lofted a high foul toward our direction. It bounced once and plopped warm and snug onto the blanket. It was a case of a Good Thing coming to a Good Person. I eyed it with awe and coveted it even more. Before I could savor the glow of a real, honest to goodness Major League Ball, albeit an American League one, Uncle Ben handed it to me.

That ball was the greatest possible gift to a 13-year-old boy more in love with Giants than Girls. Several years later I realized he had given me much more than a ball, but I waited nearly two decades before I actively acknowledged it. A month before my 32nd birthday I rode Amtrak to New Mexico. For months I had felt a need to understand my past. I rented a car, drove to Madrid, and breathlessly searched for a coal mine. The mine shrank as I explored it. The air was cool and felt nice on my skin. Family members of long ago accompanied me. The coolness I felt was theirs.

My mom lived in Madrid until she was nine. My grandparents were there and, of course, my aunts and uncles. I say of course because families stayed together then. They also moved together. They moved to escape the discrimination of a company town, to get paid in dollars rather than in scrip, to live where they wished instead of where they were confined to a section of town, the back section. They moved to California.

They spoke Spanish mostly, and the move had to be terrifying. Uncle Ben opened a TV repair shop. Another uncle got a master's degree in business. My grandmother worked in the burgeoning post-World War II aeronautics industry. But before any of that they worked in Santa Clara County's fields, picking green beans, slicing apricots, canning tomatoes. They worked hard, but when you're a kid you don't think about such things.

I think about them now, however. What dreams did my uncle have? What plans? When he left the known for its opposite, was his dream one of fame or of a fresh start, or did he simply wish to save his lungs and dignity from certain premature demise that came from coal and from those who oversaw its removal? I never asked about his dreams and now I am unable to. Ben Nieto, 85-years-old Giants fan, died three months ago.

The casket surprised me by its weight. I had never been a pallbearer before and was still apprehensive when the service began. My duties temporarily done, I looked at the faces of my family. "If you look at a thing nine hundred and ninety-nine times," G.K. Chesterton once wrote, "you are perfectly safe; if you look at it the thousandth time, you are in frightful danger of seeing it for the first time."

For the first time I saw the faces of immediate family and of distant relatives, faces joined in reverence to a man deserving of it. I saw my grandmother's frailty and was startled. I saw the gray entrenched in my mom's hair and the wrinkles inexorably working into my brother's features. I also saw my uncle's great-granddaughter. Barely a month old, she will never know the man whose funeral she slept through, but he is as much a part of her as her dreams. And as much a part of me. I am able to pursue my dreams—in this case, writing and traveling and honoring baseball's past—because of those like my uncle who have preceded me.

The church service over, we made the short drive to the cemetery I used to study so many years before. Not quite a year after finishing my journey, if a journey can ever be truly finished, I was in a cemetery once more. Again I scanned the faces of family and was briefly shattered by the knowledge that we will not always be together. I turned toward the casket and understood the priest's words in Wappingers Falls. Though death is inevitable for the obscure and for the famous, it is not final. The echoes of past generations will always fill us with life.

D.J.D.
San Leandro, California
November 1996

In the midst of winter I finally discovered within me an invincible summer.
—Albert Camus

Everything is possible to him who dares.
—Al Spalding

Their bodies are buried in peace and their name lives for ever.
—Ecclesiasticus 44:14

Dave's Route

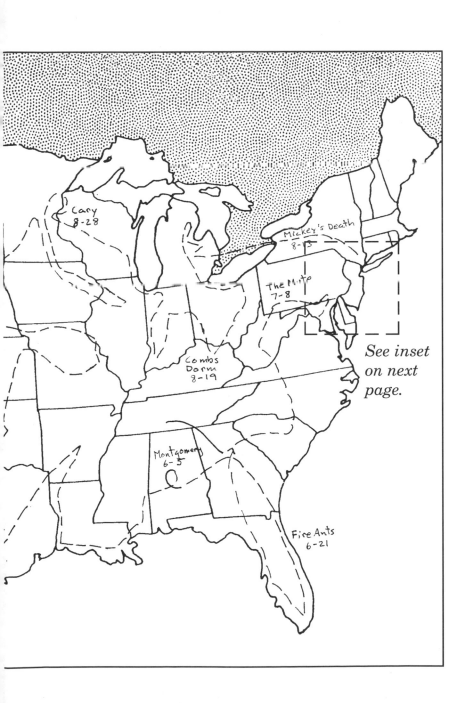

Cary
8-28

Mickey's Death
8-13

The Mitt
7-8

Combs
Dorm
8-19

See inset
on next
page.

Montgomery
6-5

Fire Ants
6-21

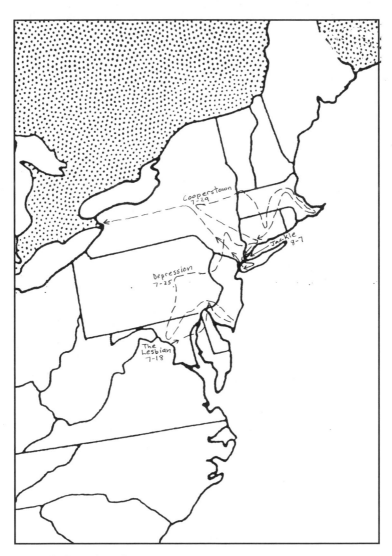

North by Northeast

DEPARTURE

When will I be there I don't know,
When will I get there I ain't certain,
All that I know is I am on my way.
—Paint Your Wagon

My boycott of the 1995 baseball season lasted into the top of the first on Opening Day. Fred McGriff faced Terry Mulholland. A day after leaving my teaching job, I turned on the radio searching for Oldies but instead got the Braves and Giants and memories of a Guatemalan garbage dump. Still angry from the strike in '94, I had vowed to ignore baseball for at least a season, but the cadence of a well-called game will always lure me. I listened and thought. What in the name of Jesus Alou was Mulholland doing back with San Francisco? Wasn't he with the Yankees last year and Philadelphia before that? Three teams in three years. Whatever happened to a team hanging on to a good southpaw?

Welcome to modern baseball, where loyalty and stability are as common as the Cubs in the World Series. I desired Oldies in more than my music. I wished I could tune in to a time of day games, grass fields, baggy wool uniforms, and domeless parks. I wished DH stood for doubleheader rather than designated hitter. I wished Ty Cobb ran the bases, not tycoons. And I wished players stayed with organizations long enough to develop recognition and affection rather than strolling from team to team like the locals surveying the *putas* in the Guatemala City dump.

Families live off of and on the refuse in the capital of Central America's largest country. In 1992, however, I saw no families, only a series of rooms. They lined the dump's edge, 15, maybe 20, in all. Copper-skinned women waited, hope as faded as their thin pastel blouses. The men roamed across fetid garbage, which made me nauseous after a few moments. They peeked in rooms, studied the women, and moved on. Like today's free agents, they searched for the best offer. And the whores, like today's owners, legs and arms open for a loveless embrace, willingly obliged.

The stench was overpowering. Decades of filth were layered in several *futbol*-sized fields of vermin, disease, rats, diapers, rotting food, and excrement. Poverty's compost pile. I left, anxious to return to my *pension*, hopefully to watch that night's All-Star Game. Blocks away, the odor was still pervasive. It had soaked into me. It was on my shirt, my pants, my shoes, my skin. I showered, and washed my clothes two, three, four times. Finally, only my Asics reeked. They were saturated with the smell and I eventually tossed them aside. I wanted to do the same with baseball. Toss it aside like a pair of foul-smelling footwear that no longer served a purpose. But even though baseball reeked these days, it had penetrated me too fully. I was determined to fight its hold, and I realized that on this trip to find the past by forgetting the present I could still retaliate. Baseball's grip wasn't that strong. I found the Oldies station, and the next day I read that Mulholland got hammered and the Giants, my beloved Giants who I'd followed for 26 years, lost. For them it was the beginning of a season that belonged in the garbage dump and I tried to act as though that didn't bother me a bit.

2

THE IDEA

A fixed idea ends in foolishness or heroism.
—Victor Hugo

Who knows where ideas come from? Does God snap His fingers and they appear, like suddenly finding your keys on the kitchen table? Do nature's forces rise together and create them from some sort of miniature (but no less cosmic) big bang? Is it just random luck? My idea came in the summer of 1991 during a casual trip to a used bookstore in Berkeley, California, with my friend Jude. She was in fiction, while I was in sports, perusing a copy of *The Whole Baseball Catalogue*, an eclectic grouping of baseball significa.

A photo of Satchel Paige's grave caught my eye. It had a question mark on the spot reserved for a birthdate. Maybe Satchel really was ageless. Then, I

read about William Hulbert's grave. A stone baseball
served as the marker. The graves were unique and as
different as, well, white and black. Hulbert, wealthy,
tyrannical, strongheaded, was the force behind the
creation of the National League. The easygoing but
shrewd and strong-armed Paige was kept out of the
Major Leagues until he was well into his 40s. If figures
as disparate as these had such fascinating graves,
what about the others? I studied a list of players and
their burial sites, players I had heard of and dreamed
of since childhood. Ruth in Hawthorne, New York;
Cobb in Royston, Georgia; and Josh Gibson in Pittsburgh. What must those gravesites look like? And
Dizzy Dean in Bond, Mississippi, I had to see that. I
could trek around the country, combining my love of
travel and baseball and the past.

Perhaps because I teach eighth-grade American
History, the past is such a crucial element in my life. By
the late-1980s, baseball was already bothering me. The
focus on money and the disregard of individuals who
built the game were commonplace. My attention to
modern baseball waned so I threw myself into the
game's history. I read and learned and remembered
and fell in love again. A tour of the gravesites would be
an extension of my renewed devotion. I would pay
homage to Honus, give respects to Rogers, mourn at
Grove's grave.

The idea was exciting, but I debated whether I
should buy the book. I'm cheap and thought I could
save $5 by copying the list by hand. Jude came over
and I explained my hesitation. Her positive outlook
and directness are a bit like brocolli. They're good for

me, but I sometimes find them hard to swallow and avoid them for weeks. Her high-pitched voice was stern and admonishing. I bought the book. Friends learned of my plans and were supportive. But like so many other dreams—triathlons, new languages, political office—this one was soon on the shelf.

Until 1994. With the strike and cancellation of the World Series, baseball had had a bad year. It was a .195 batting average with 45 errors at short bad year, a torn rotator cuff bad year. But baseball wasn't alone in suffering through 1994. I had my own year of crises. A pair of painful romantic relationships, problems at work, the loss of $22,000, half my life savings, in one of the state's biggest investment fraud scams, and my parents' unexpected divorce. The events devastated me and I turned to baseball for solace. I went to A's games whenever I could; they played as badly as I felt. Then I dusted off my nearly four-year-old dream of seeing the gravesites. If I were to be battered by the events of daily life, then I would attack life myself. If I were to be pummeled, at least I'd be on the offensive instead of resting blandly at home, which was undoubtedly good news to the mute who assaulted me in Charleroi, Pennsylvania.

The school district granted a leave of absence more readily than I was comfortable with. Beware of those too anxious to see you off. My teaching year ended April 25 and I departed the following day which, appropriately, was the beginning of the 1995 season.

I felt that people thought I was running away from my problems, and at age 34 maybe I was. The journey, however, had evolved into something more significant than idle wanderings in the nation's cemeteries. What it had become I couldn't answer in spoken words. Only in silence or on paper. Why are you doing this? What exactly are you going to do? Why now? Some questions do not permit easy answers, and easy answers are the only ones we allow time for. We can understand speechlessness, we can even take time to read, but for a thorough explanation, for the necessary details to get your thoughts across, we need hours, an afternoon, a day, the right moment. When did you have any of those? When did I?

3

NELLIE AND
THE DEMONS

*And I'd made up my mind that I was going to be a
baseball player. At least I was going to give it my best
shot, give myself every chance, and not ever have to be
one of those frustrated athletes who goes through life
wondering what might have been.*
—Frank McCormick

The route to St. Paul, Nebraska, Grover Cleveland
Alexander's burial site and my first grave, was as direct as a well-thrown knuckleball. A number of inter-
mediary stops were necessary, including my mom in
Santa Cruz, California, and my dad in Las Vegas. My
vehicle was a 1993 red Geo Metro with a lousy radio
and no air conditioning. I named it Nellie in honor of
Nellie Bly, the crusading stunt journalist of the late
1800s, and Nellie Fox, the White Sox second baseman
who was finally elected to the Hall in 1997. Nellie was
small but fiercely economical. Her three cylinders

8

Photo by Lori Milstein.

would provide great gas mileage and I hoped they could handle the various mountain ranges ahead. The Rockies were the first test. Much of the ascent was made in third gear at 35 miles per hour but Nellie endured. I ultimately drove 25,873 miles in snow, hail, thunderstorms, and heat waves. While driving through 43 states, Nellie was unfailingly faithful, as reliable as her namesakes, one who navigated her way around the world in 72 days and the other who once played in 798 straight games.

But when I left Denver on the morning of May 4, I was worried about Nellie's ability to handle the trek. Even more, I was worried about my own. Normally I would have smothered my fears with food and music, a pair of national pastimes that too often subvert introspection. We drown thoughts in calories, TV, tunes, a million other things, anything really, to keep us from ourselves. We fear ourselves because we fear what we

see when we look too closely. We fear what remains
once we're beyond the show and attitude and defenses
and whatever else we build for protection. After all, no
one looks good in a closeup, not with the pores distorted
into a beehive and blemishes magnified into Badlands
National Park. We each construct our own Green Monster to hide the monster within. Although I intended to
travel solo, my demons hitched a ride.

Sometimes they shouted but usually their messages came in random whispers. Regardless, they always sounded the same. "You can't do this. The country
is too vast, you are too little, this is something for
Steinbeck." Ah, Steinbeck. *Travels With Charley* still
inspires me. Any confusion between Steinbeck and me,
however, is purely halluciogenic. Yes, I am traveling
the U.S. And yes, I have named my car. But Steinbeck?
You might as well slap a stick in my hands and call me
The Splendid Splinter. Or strip me naked, douse my
body with marble dust, and pass me off as Michel-
angelo's David. (Hmmm, maybe we're onto something
there.) Steinbeck was a big, mighty man, a man's man,
a tough, hearty beef stew of a man. Me? May I have
seconds on the Pad Thai, please, and another slice of
lemon for my water?

The trip would be a challenge, and part of that
meant listening to the demons. I vowed to not block
their voices; I wanted to confront them, learn from
them, deal with them, like Thoreau dealt with life in
his cabin. The demons would have their say. But time
and again I sought to stop them, instinctively reaching
for the beef jerky beside me or to the radio ahead, although I hungered for neither food nor music. I would

catch myself in time and return to my thoughts. The morning was lovely, the Rockies behind, and adventure in front, as I sped across the Interstate to Nebraska,

After 45 miles I wondered why I had yet to see signs for Sterling, tucked in Colorado's northeastern corner. I checked the map as I drove, searching for Limon on I-76, the town I had seen signs for. It was nowhere near Sterling. It was on I-70 and so was I. I was on the wrong freeway, heading toward Kansas and had added two hours by carelessness. The voices laughed and sneered and jeered as I pulled off the road to plot a new course. I grabbed a slab of jerkey, jammed it into my mouth, and flicked on the radio. "Highway to Hell" was playing.

4

THE FAVORED
SON—SCORNED

*I don't feel sorry for myself or excuse my drinking.
I just had two strikes on me when I came into the
world. My father back in Nebraska was a hard
drinker before me, and so was my grandfather before
him. Sure I tried to stop—I just couldn't.*
—Grover Cleveland Alexander

I spent the night in Arnold, Nebraska, camping at
a state recreation area. When I awoke the tent was
dewed over, and I worried it would sour if I bundled it
up. Instead I let it loose like a dead spider and headed
for St. Paul 92 miles away. The mist, coupled with my
blurred eyes from a lack of sleep (I was sure I would be
knifed during the night), gave Nebraska's mid-section
a Dali-esque look. The hills were figments that disappeared if you tried touching them. I looked warily at
the expansive, angular sprinklers, which appeared as

12

loose-limbed praying mantises waiting to pounce. And the road reached impossibly far to the horizon as though it were chewing gum stretched by mischievous fingers. The clouds were too low and the black and yellow, triangular No Passing Zone signs looked like they meant it. The situation was surreal. What was I doing on Eastbound 92 in Nebraska on a school day?

My eighth-grade U.S. History students at Bancroft Middle School in San Leandro, California (only five minutes from the Oakland Coliseum), were asking the same question. Leaving them was painful. My emotions ricocheted between excitement and guilt before settling on guilt. I shouldn't have felt bad, though, after a former student tried to gun me down with a semiautomatic the previous night. That was the most recent dream. The most painful one occurred earlier in the week. I was at a riverbank with three students from my fourth-period class. An alligator surfaced in the distance as we rinsed gold tokens we had found. Two students moved to higher ground. I joined them, giving no warning to the 14-year-old eastern European immigrant who remained at the water's edge. The alligator swooped upon the boy, biting him in half as I looked benignly on. A few students deserve death by reptile, but this boy—kind, quiet, respectful—is not among them.

I feared I had cursed my trip by not finishing the school year. St. Paul, with its 2,009 residents, two flashing red lights, and gregarious mayor who owned and ran a burger joint on the edge of town, was my first stop. It would have made more sense to visit California graves first, but I wanted something different at the beginning. As nervous and as uncertain as a newlywed (or at least as newlyweds used to be), I strolled into the Uptown Grill on Howard Avenue, sat at the counter, and waited for I wasn't sure what. Minutes later a dairy farmer sat beside me and rambled from topic to topic as though we were old friends, even telling me he had purchased several kegs of beer for that weekend's high school graduation party. When he finally asked what I was doing in town, he directed me to the Dodge shop across the street where Franklin Alexander spends most of his days.

"So, Grover Cleveland Alexander was your uncle?"
"Yes, that's right."
"Your father and he were brothers?"
"Yes, but my father wasn't into drinking."
This wasn't going as I had hoped. Alex was a pasty-faced, fleshy man in his 70s who was stingy with information. He insisted that I sit; I did. He remained standing. Where was the easygoing old-timer I hoped to find? Where was the life-long resident who breathed anecdotes? I persisted.
"Did you spend much time with him?"
"Oh, sure. We hunted and fished....(H)e had his regular crew here and his bootleg whiskey down by the river." Alex said he often led his staggering uncle home after dusk. He was frequently drunk but that "was his business."
Was it? It was an appropriate question to consider a few days after Michigan football coach Gary Moeller

resigned because of his drunken tantrum in a restaurant. I found a copy of the Omaha paper and read that University of Nebraska football coach Tom Osborne defended Moeller:

"Twenty years ago, and even 15 years ago, if someone had behaved like that it might have been swept under the rug or tolerated. But because of the visibility of college athletics today, anytime anything with a major college coach gets involved, it gets big publicity. There was a time when things were handled in-house. The police might have taken him home and even the president of the university wouldn't know about it."

Should it matter what athletes do after hours? Do we judge too harshly? Would Alexander have lasted as long as he did under contemporary conditions?

His niece, an 81-year-old named Elma, said things would have been different for her Uncle Dode, a childhood name, had he been a modern ballplayer. He would have received help today. None was available years ago. She is sympathetic to Grover and proudly shares scrapbooks and information of her famous relative with strangers. I sat at her kitchen table reading articles of long ago. She recalled him fondly, describing how he perfected his pinpoint control by hurling rocks at chickens and how her family surrounded a radio in 1926 and listened to him fan Lazerri, the most famous strikeout in World Series history.

Elma left the kitchen to retrieve more memorabilia. I was uncomfortable. It was a mistake for an old woman to let a strange man into her home. I felt my presence was a crime and expected the police or a neighbor or a passerby to rescue Elma from her foolishness and trust.

But that's how these people live. Another woman, this
one 75, aging, arthritic, and amiable, invited me into
her home because of storm warnings. As I listened to
the rain that night, laying in a bed rather than a tent,
I thought how vulnerable this woman was. If I chose
to, I could rob her, harm her, even kill her. Nonetheless, I appreciated her trust and tried to sleep. But I
couldn't. Now wide-awake, I realized she wasn't the
only vulnerable one. She could rob me, harm me, even
kill me. What was I doing in the home of a woman I
didn't know?

Surviving the hospitality, I biked to Elmwood Cemetery the next morning. It's on the edge of town only a
half-mile from Grover Cleveland Alexander Ballpark.
The plot was unremarkable: a war veteran's off-white
headstone, synthetic flowers, two red plastic bats, and
a plastic ball. A bronze plaque noted his 1938 enshrine-
ment into the Hall. It covered his date of death, which
had been incorrectly engraved. If you can add insult to
death, the town had done so, just as it added insult to
his final years of life.

Alexander's drinking was legendary. It worsened after World War I because of shell shock and epilepsy. His public drunkenness made him an outcast in the town that once lauded him as Alex the Great. Eventually his bar tab was cut off and, because of cancer, so was an ear. He took a room in a boarding house. He was broke. Ol' Low and Away was Down and Out. On November 4, 1950, he died in his room. He was alone.

How could this place, which had been so welcoming to me, be so cruel to its most famous citizen? St. Paul's kindness must be built on conformity, I thought, as I sat in the St. Paul High School gymnasium for graduation. A student rose and prayed. A counselor assured me that the prayer was constitutional because all 47 graduates supported it. I doubted that a lone Muslim's or Jew's or, God forbid, an atheist's views would be tolerated in this small, white, Christian, agricultural community.

But I misjudged the students. They marched out to Pink Floyd's "We Don't Need No Education." They somersaulted and hopped and cartwheeled and danced down the aisles. They wore sunglasses and funny hats. Maybe conformity wasn't such a big deal in this area.

Another high school graduation, this one in nearby Elba, Grover's birthplace, was held the following day. Ten students graduated, double the number in the Class of '94 whose five members—all boys—landed on "The Tonight Show," said the principal, because of their inability to select a prom queen.

Several slides were shown of each student, from infancy to senior picture. It was a nice final touch before the students entered their chosen field, which in the case of most was to eventually work in the field. After the ceremony, families left hurriedly. I followed several cars, wondering where the action was. They led me to a bar, a small place where you could get a beer. The name on the sign was familiar: Grover's.

5

JAKE (JACK?) BECKLEY (BECKMAN?)

Fame is a vapor; popularity an accident; the only earthly certainty is oblivion.
—Mark Twain

"Hi, I'm trying to get some information on Jake Beckley. He's a Hall-of-Fame baseball player who's buried here."

"Jack Beckley? Oh, sure."

This was Twain country—Hannibal, Missouri—where Beckley could have starred in any number of stories, including the famous, turn-of-the-century ballplayer who gets as much respect and attention as roadkill. Hannibal is clearly Twain's town. Beckley is a dismissed interloper, resigned to playing second fiddle if only they'd get him a fiddle.

The information lady directed me to a stone marker amidst the irritating jumbalaya of overblown

Twainism. I passed Becky Thatcher's house, young
Samuel's dad's law office, the infamous white fence.
Jake's marker abutted a parking lot and was gradually
disappearing behind imperialistic shrubs. Ol' Eagle
Eye's eyes looked toward the pavement and the
Hickory Stick Gift Shop. I had the feeling that if I re-
turned in six or seven years, the marker would be used
as a parking curb.

My knowledge of Jake was limited. I checked my
Baseball Encyclopedia for help and went to the library
for back issues of the *Hannibal Courier-Post*. I found
them, but first uncovered a city councilman who knew
everything about Jake, including his tombstone's location in Mt. Olivet Cemetery.

"But according to my records," I said, "he's in Riverside."

"He was there but they moved him."

"Are you sure?"

"Definitely. I can draw you a map."

Pleased with my luck, I turned to the huge chunks
of the past bound in volumes. They lay horizontally and
were as brittle as a great-grandparent. I'll be sure to
never move granny as I did the volumes. The 1918 book
was on the bottom, and I slid it off with the care I give
yesterday's newspaper. To my horror dozens of yel-
lowed scraps floated to the carpet. What if you picked
Grandma off the couch and saw an ear drop off. A toe.
A tooth. A finger.

Two women at Mt. Olivet scurried to find information. They checked computer files, 3 x 5 cards, and
burial records.

"I'm sorry," said one, "we don't have any Jake Beckman."

"Beckley."

The other woman was puzzled. "I don't remember him being moved." She was kind, and I felt sorry for her. She was fat. Heaps of flesh bounced and sagged as she moved. Viewed as moral failures incapable of self control, obese people don't stand a chance in America.

They'd be much better off in a Latin country where there's a healthier attitude toward fat. I once got on a bus with an overweight female friend. The driver shouted for passengers to move so *la gordita* (the fat woman) could sit. It was simply a description, not an insult (although you couldn't tell my friend that). Red hair. Brown eyes. Fat butt. They all describe.

The fat woman (and only by acknowledging it can we stop the stigma) found a book which confirmed Beckley's location at Riverside, not Mt. Olivet. She drew me a map. As I drove to Riverside, clouds darkened. During the previous week I'd grown watchful and respectful of the weather, having endured snow flurries in the Rockies, thunderstorms in Nebraska, and floods in Missouri. I passed old homes, much more indicative of long ago Mississippi River life than the silly stores which Twain surely would have satirized. By time I passed Lover's Leap, the supposed death site of a Native American Romeo and Juliet, the first nice weather of the trip was gone.

I turned onto a pitted dirt and rock road. The No Hunting signs seemed particularly emphatic. As I drove up a steep hill lightning cracked, sounding like Jake whipping one of his 243 career triples, fourth on the all-time list. (Don't groan, this is a baseball odyssey.) I reached the fence ("That's the Jewish section," the woman had said. "You don't want it.") as the most severe storm of the trip broke. My umbrella gave little protection during the 30 yards I walked. When I saw the family marker, the rain stopped as though an umpiring crew had ordered it. Jake was to the left of his parents, Rosine and Bernhard. I retrieved my drawing materials and lawn chair from the car.

The sun returned as I sketched the grave. The warmth dried me. I was happy and bemused. I felt guided by God, by the elements, and, who knows, maybe by Jake's spirit. The misinformation I'd received at the library was fortuitous. Riverside was what I came to know as a dead cemetery. No office, no workers, isolated from help. Had I gone there first, lacking the directions of the fat woman from Mt. Olivet, I would have spent hours combing through graves in a frustrating search. There'd be enough opportunities for that, I would discover.

I still didn't know a lot about Jake but I had a hunch that he would have fit in well with Twain—easygoing, wry, caustic, able to give and take a joke, appreciative of irony. I certainly hoped so because when I returned downtown for a final look at his marker, a white stream of birdshit flowed from the corner of Ol' Eagle Eye's beak.

6

SUNNY JIM'S MASSEUSE

*They proceed further into money-making, and
the more they value it, the less they value virtue.
Or aren't virtue and wealth so opposed that if
they were set on scales, they'd always incline
in opposite directions?*
—Plato

Potato sacks served as wallpaper. Old saws, painted with serene agricultural settings, hung above, as did horseshoes, iron kettles, and cleavers. Nine propellar planes made from Coke and Pepsi cans flew overhead, suspended by string and plastic clothespins hooked to the ceiling. I'd been told to try Homer's BBQ for the atmosphere as much as the food. "It's *National Geographic* 1968," said a man, although it looked more like *Farmers Weekly* 1947.

The diner was off old Route 66 in Sullivan, Missouri, the final stop for Sunny Jim Bottomley, so named because of his unbridled enthusiasm. Jim should have willed some of his cheerfulness to a handful of boys I met in a baseball card shop in town. They couldn't comprehend why anyone would willingly come to Sullivan, an hour's drive from St. Louis.

I was eager to meet Homer who, I was told, could talk for hours to anyone. I'm envious of such people, those who can converse with strangers with the ease it takes to chew. The lack of self-consciousness and the irrelevancy of the audience are glorious. I wanted to see what he knew about Sunny Jim, but first ordered a hickory-smoked chuck burger and my standard glass of water, the only beverage I drank in a restaurant the entire trip save for the strawberry daiquiri that was ridiculed in Gettysburg.

"We have the best water in the world," said Homer, heading to the kitchen.

A customer and I discussed the merits of Sullivan water. "Not much bacteria or lead," he proudly pointed out. How much was not much? I looked at my water for signs of life when a sauce-smeared burger arrived. It wasn't what I expected and I eyed it suspiciously.

"What about that virus in Africa?" Homer blurted to any receptive listener. Aha, a conversation starter. The day before I had perused a blurb in *Newsweek* on the deadly Ebola virus.

"What's that?" asked the customer.

"It's called Ebola," I said, picking up my burger. "It makes you bleed from the eyes, ears, and nose. You bleed to death in a short time."

I took a bite; it was great. Homer, meanwhile, shook catsup from a two-gallon can onto his fried potatoes. "Then it pops the skin right off," he said. "It's terrible."

The topic of tragic African viruses exhausted, I asked about Bottomley. "I was told you might know something about him."

"I used to rub Sunny Jim's legs," said Homer. "We had to rub up, like this, toward the heart. He'd pay us a nickel." The thought of this old man as a young boy was tough enough to fathom. Thinking of him as Bottomley's masseuse was bizarre.

"How'd he treat you?"

"We were poor folk and he treated us just regular."

"What would he think of today's ballplayers?"

"He always said to get as much out of the game as you can."

With an average salary of $1.1 million a year, today's players have taken him at his word. In 1970 I was in fifth grade and did a report on the highest-paid ballplayers and only two, Mays and Yaz, I think, topped the magical $100,000 mark. Dimaggio made just over $700,000 in his entire career, and it was probably harder to get that than face his nemesis, Cleveland's Mel Harder. The average salary in baseball used to be six or seven times that of the average worker. Now it's about 50 times greater.

I thought of another first baseman known for his disposition, Will Clark, who once was my favorite player. I loved watching him with the Giants—the glare, the attitude, the swing, the '89 playoffs against the Cubs, the stony jaw. He was a throwback. Sure, he was making his two or three million but he was worth it, and I was sure money was not his motivation. No way. He played for the love of the game. And then came the salary dispute after the 1993 season. Clark was coming off back-to-back, less than thrilling seasons. The Giants offered something like $14 million over three years, but he jumped to Texas, whose package had better wrapping. Throwback? I wanted to throw up.

"It used to be the rich would watch the poor," said Homer, "now the poor watch the rich."

Perhaps, but in this season of discontent I'd been hearing that thousands of the poor and middle class were staying home and it wasn't because of an obscure Third World virus. Declining attendance and fan displeasure seemed to have gotten the players' attention. If Sunny Jim were playing today, even he would have trouble finding something to smile about.

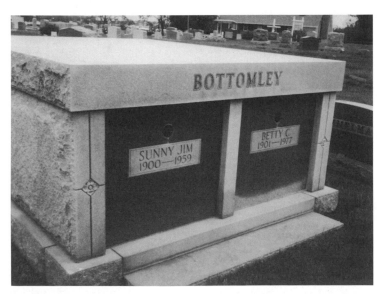

7

STRANGLED HISTORY

*Sometimes you're the windshield, sometimes
you're the bug, Sometimes you're the Louisville
Slugger, baby, sometimes you're the ball.*
—Mary Chapin Carpenter

John Brown was my grandfather. As a child I felt
he was somehow *the* John Brown, the radical abolition-
ist, a catalyst to the Civil War. Grandpa was born in
1905, so the birthdates didn't match (they were more
than a century apart) but that didn't deter me. That
the two were as physically different as Stan Musial
and Stan Laurel was also no concern. Grandpa was
half black and half Choctaw Indian with a stocky, formidable build carved from the New Mexico coal fields.
He could have doubled for Roy Campanella. His namesake was angular, harsh as a whip, severe as a Kansas
winter, and had 20 children by two wives. I couldn't
understand where my mom fit among his kids when

she only had a brother and sister that I knew of. Where were the others?

Grandpa's eyes melted with kindness and he had an inexhaustible supply of Tahitian Punch and ice cream. The other John Brown would be more apt to give you a punch, or even hack you into pieces, which is what he and four of his sons did to five pro-slavery advocates in Pottawatomie, Kansas, in 1856.

I never tried to reconcile Grandpa's kind eyes with his role in Bleeding Kansas or the Harper's Ferry raid or his hanging, although those acts made me cautious in knocking the bedpost when his snoring kept me awake nights in the room we sometimes shared. I never thought to ask about his apparent reincarnation. Even then, I sensed there were family secrets one wasn't to disturb. If he wished to unveil his past he would. The revelation that Grandpa was not a crazed martyr came sometime between life's two most painful discoveries: the non-existence of Santa Claus and the impossibility of a Major League career.

Now I wished I had asked about the name. Did you like it? Were you named after John Brown? What did you think of him? Did it change you?

An hour southwest of Kansas City, I was lured by signs of Brown's cabin in Oswatomie, the starting point of his bloody raids. The local museum was closed, as was the one at the cabin. A silly statue of Brown stood in the park. My access to the past shut off, I was frustrated that more wasn't being done to preserve history. That is the job of small cities. They must do something more than open an antique mall or post signs that read, "Historic District—One Mile," or sell tickets for

the 75th Annual John Brown Jamboree. Notable figures are trivialized into nothingness at best and cari-
catures at worst. In 2095, Oklahoma City will no doubt
host the 100th Annual Federal Building Festivities.
"It's a Real Blast" the posters will assure us. When the
past is ignored or forgotten or manipulated, a nation
becomes rootless, a lost balloon.

I wondered if my anger was a result of the weather.
It was my first exposure to humidity since leaving
three weeks before. Invisible clammy hands pressed
against me and I felt formaldehyde oozing from my
pores. I dared touch nothing because of the dishearten-
ing stickiness upon removal. If I was this miserable in
mid-May in Kansas after seeing eight graves, how
could I tolerate the East Coast in the heat and humidity of summer? Maybe I should have gotten air conditioning after all. Had it only been three hours since my
last shower?

The assault on the past continued in Winfield, Kansas, where Fred Clarke, the Pirate outfielder and manager, is buried. His parents were morally opposed to
young Fred getting money for playing ball. (Did Mr.
and Mrs. Bonds have the same qualms? Or Mrs. Sand-
ers: "Now Deion, I don't want you playing no pro ball. I
don't want you associating with none of those men.
They aren't gentlemanly. They cuss, they got bigger
heads than Barney, and don't dance too good." "But
Mama, $3 trillion and all the gold I can wear!" "OK,
son, but make sure the bonus is up-front and the incen-
tives within reach and tax-free.")

Like Deion, Clarke knew the value of a buck. Actually, he knew the value of one hundred of them. As a 17-year-old, he was promised $100 when reporting to Louisville in 1894.

"I asked the manager, Billy Barnie, 'Where's my money?'"

"Oh, you'll get that after the game."

"I want it now."

Barnie offered a check. "OK," said Clarke, "if you cash it." Clarke played the game with five $20 bills safety pinned to the inside of his uniform.

The money would be useful now to clean Clarke's grave. Clarke and his wife are set away from the mass of monuments in St. Mary's Cemetery. Berry-eating birds had crapped prolifically on the grave of a man who at the turn of the century was as well known in Pittsburgh as Carnegie. A purple, white, and brown crust topped the marker. It looked like it had not been visited since his death in August 1960 in the midst of the Pirates' great pennant run.

It was the first neglected grave I had seen. It foreshadowed those I saw in Florida and left me depressed. I pedaled away and foolishly stopped at the city's Veterans Memorial. It told that, during the Mexican-American War, "the stars and stripes advanced to a new frontier extending the domain of freedom." The interpretation was a generous one. The extension of slavery in some areas and the appropriation of land in others were among the freedoms advanced.

The memorial then informed me how the United States leapt to aid the oppressed in the Spanish-American War because a "call of human justice shall not go unheeded nor an encroachment of human rights unchallenged." A black teenage boy strolled by. Were his ancestors' calls heeded or were the lines inevitably busy? Better get call-waiting, son.

The manipulation of facts like items from a magician's bag of tricks drove me into a frenzy. Facts should be sacred, not a remote control train you pick up on the way from work so you have something to maneuver at will. A Baby Ruth commercial had aired recently. Images of the Babe floated throughout it, even though the candy was named after President Cleveland's infant daughter—Bambina, not Bambino. (This was only minor foreshadowing to the summer's true folly concerning Ruth—the city of Baltimore's nine-foot, 800-pound bronze statue of the left-handed Babe holding a righty's glove to his hip. The sculptor's pained response: "It was the right glove on the wrong man or the wrong glove on the right man." Or the wrong artist for the right man.)

I scurried out of Winfield, driving south on Route 77 toward Oklahoma. Looking back upon my day was no better than looking through my windshield. Bugsplattered and battered, it looked how I felt. Sticky and dirty and smeared. I needed a shower but that was still two days away—at a cousin's in Oklahoma City. I was still 10 days from realizing the benefits of Holiday Inn swimming pools.

Cloud cover gave the moon a droopy-eyed look. I'd driven only 10 minutes when I saw stadium lights in Arkansas City. El Dorado and Augusta high schools were playing for the league title and a spot in the state tournament. During the trip I stopped dozens of times for games. Major league, minor league, Colt, Little League, slow-pitch. Each game was enjoyable, morsels of food to a glutton.

Parents were unusually sportsmanlike and the players hustled and cheered. I rooted for neither team until the El Dorado pitcher whined about a ball call. He stomped from the mound. "Where'd it miss? Where did that miss?" The catcher blocked his progress. "I was only asking where the ball was," he whined.

Two innings later everyone knew where one of his balls was—over the fence on a grand slam by a catcher headed to nearby powerhouse Wichita State. The slam erased a 5-4 lead. It's not often you witness poor behavior and, moments later, a well-deserved comeuppance. The day didn't seem so bad after all.

8

SAINTLY IRREVERENCE.

That best portion of a good man's life,
His little, nameless, unremembered acts
Of kindness and of love.
—William Wordsworth

A plot salesman in Kansas City told me that people often buy more, uh, real estate than they intend to use. Kid Nichols, for example, purchased three plots but uses only two. "Space is important," said the salesman. "It allows them to stretch out." He also explained the maplike grid of pathways often used in graveyards. When Kansas City's Mt. Moriah Cemetery was built in 1922, it was considered bad luck to walk over the dead.

I don't know about luck, but it sure seemed disrespectful. And then I met a black man named Jamal. He too sells plots, but at Oklahoma City's Rose Hill Cemetery. He volunteered to help me find Lloyd Waner, who we located easily.

"Shit, he's in the Hall of Fame," said Jamal. "Goddamn, I didn't know that."

It was noteworthy, I said, how few acknowledged their Hall of Fame membership on their graves. The lone statistic on Lloyd's grave was his 53 years of marriage, which might be tougher than hitting in 53 straight.

We sat on tombstones and talked. A congregation of one, I was fascinated by this reverend's irreverence. He was a rarity, an updated version of Eliza Doolittle's father in *My Fair Lady*, a man with opinions and his own moral code, and the courage to express them.

"I don't want to be disrespectful," he said, "but there are a lot of dirty, rotten cocksuckers in this place. Maybe we're sitting on one now." He looked down in contemplation and added, "If the shoe doesn't fit, sorry."

Jamal speculated what the markers would say if only the truth were included: "Here lies Uncle Harry. He let his kids go hungry and played the horses and whores." Eulogies would surely be different.

Jamal grew up in New York City and left home at 14. "I did some drugs, had some run-ins with the law but nothing serious." He spoke as though he were on a time limit and had only a few seconds left. For an hour he talked, as blunt as Cosell, as eloquent as King, as profane as Pryor.

He expounded on capitalism, sales techniques, race relations, and the vanity of the monuments he sells: "Even though I like the workmanship, the aesthetic, it's fucking nuts." He apparently fuels up on ideas during the many hours he spends thinking among the dead. The cemetery provides him peace and solitude.

"People ask, 'Aren't you scared?' Hell, no. There's no one out here to hurt me. I'm worried about the people on two legs. And if one of them comes out of the grave, I'm gonna ask, 'How'd you do that?'"

Hunger and the mid-afternoon heat made me tired. Jamal either noticed or stopped because I no longer fed him questions like quarters popped into a jukebox. He left and I sketched the grave. Why weren't Paul (buried in Florida) and Lloyd interred together? George and Harry Wright were also in separate cemeteries. (Obviously the brothers who play together don't...) Forty-five minutes later I walked to my car, anxious for a nap, some food, and a shower.

Jamal drove toward me and I cringed. I liked him but didn't have the energy for more conversation.

Oklahoma City, OK   May 17, 1995

WANER

FRANCES MAE   LLOYD JAMES
MAY 27   NOV. 11 (53)   MAR. 16   JULY 22
1909   1989   YRS   1906   1982

There was no way to avoid him and I braced for the verbal onslaught. He pulled alongside me and thrust his hand out the window. A large Styrofoam cup filled with ice and a chilled bottle of Crystal Geyser. "I thought you could use this."

A cup of ice. A bottle of cold water.

A saint.

9

UMW MEETS MLBPA

When I was twelve years old I was working in the mines from seven in the morning to seven at night, six days a week. Which means a seventy-two-hour week, if you care to figure it up. For those 72 hours I got $3.75. About five cents an hour. There was nothing strange in those days about a twelve year old Polish kid in the mines for 72 hours a week at a nickel an hour. What was strange was that I ever got out of there.
—Stanley Coveleski

This being regarded as a Star Pitcher is a harder job than being a coal miner.
—Ed Walsh

The setting—an imaginary meeting of union members of the United Mine Workers and the Major League Baseball Players Association to promote information, respect, sensitivity, and camaraderie between two historically exploited labor organizations. The

meeting takes place at the community center in McAlester, Oklahoma, burial place of Iron Man Joe McGinnity, the Orioles' and Giants' star pitcher at the turn of the century and a former coal miner. Nearly all of the miners' dialogue is taken from oral histories of McAlester miners.

Miner 1: Howdy, m'names Joe Sullivan. UMW 731. Glad you could make it.

Player 1: Uh, don't you wash your hands? You been working on your jag? That oil smeared on you?

M 1: No, sir. Coal dust. Gets in ya like you're a sponge. Near impossible to clear totally out. My wife washes my work clothes 'til her hands bleed. Gets 'em clean, but her hands are a sight. Say, what team you play for?

P 1: Braves. Would you like my autograph? Normally I charge $20 but since we're cooperating and all, how about $15?

M 1: Don't much know what I'd do with an autograph. Even if I did, couldn't truly afford it. We load about 20 ton a day an' make $5 or $6 a day. An' that's for three of us.

P 1: Well, the greenbacks went a helluva lot further back then. No capital gains. Try getting by on one point two million when you owe alimony to two wives...

Miner 2: Two wives?

P 1: Well, two ex-wives. So you owe alimony to your ex-wives and your girlfriend thinks the Mastercard is the greatest thing since free agency, plus making two house payments.

M 1: What do you need two houses for?

P 1: Because I made too much last year.

M 2: You made too much?

P 1: Yup, with my $300,000 bonus for hitting my weight—and don't think that was any piece of cake because I was a little heavier this year because I, uh, had a little too much cake in the off-season, if you know what I mean, heh, heh. I had to shelter some of my dough. Then management is hell, always trying to cut our salaries. A man's got to be concerned.

M 1: Our concern sometimes is just having shelter. I know what you mean about management. They don't care what goes on. As long as you don't get the mules killed. They could replace a man, but if you lost a mule that was a disaster. They could hire another man but had to buy a mule.

Player 2: Mule Skowron. Now there was a ballplayer.

M 2: Wasn't it Moose?

P 2: Mule Moose? Don't think so. Anyway, he was as tough as they came. Played through injuries that would have put a lesser man down.

M 2: Oh, hello, dear. Gentlemen, this is my wife, Elizabeth. Dear, didn't your grandfather have a few injuries?

Woman 1: Oh, yes, my grandpa started to work in the mine in the year 1913, he was 15-years-old. He retired in the year 1958 because he was injured for the third and last time. His leg was broken, his ribs were broken, his nose was broken, and his back was hurt. The head injury caused him to lose his hearing because of nerve damage.

P 2: Ouch. I know how that feels. I got beaned in the head by the Ryan Express my rookie year and heard bells until I was eligible for arbitration. Never saw the pitch coming.

M 1: My dad got pieces of steel and sulfur in his eyes several times and he accepted it as part of the risk taken by coal miners.

P 2: Like playing at the "Stick."

M 1: The Stick?

P 2: The Stick. Candlestick Park where the Giants play. That wind blows and swirls and kicks dirt around homeplate like a wild cleaning lady and stings like the Dickens when it gets in your eyes.

W 1: Cousin Walter need only half worry about that. Walter was firing shots at Blanco when a defective fuse went off in his face. One of his eyes was blown out, a piece of coal pushed up against his brain, and a hole was blown threw his leg. He never worked in the mines again.

P 2: Ever tear a hamstring? Sounds just like notebook paper ripping in half. That nearly put me out of the show. And now the damn ownership's trying to put all of us out. Thank God for the Union.

M 1: Yes, the Union is important. I joined the Union way a back in the '30s and still belong to the United

Mine Workers. I pay my dues and draw the miners' pension. I draw the black lung pension.

P 2: Black lung. Hey, there's a thought. Wonder if they can come up with a rotator cuff pension. When that soupbone goes, you can forget the golf and tennis. Might as well not even join the country club.

M 2: I don't think you understand. Black Lung changes your entire life. It's devastating to the miner and his family.

P 1: Well, I don't know too much about that, but I do know you have two lungs but only one throwing arm.

Woman 2: If you had any idea what life was like in the mines, you would not talk as you do. When I was a little girl, a terrible explosion rocked the mine. All 30 miners were killed. My mother, my little brother Mike, and I did not know about the explosion until the next morning. A friend came and told us. It was a freezing cold day as we stood outside the mine waiting.

The explosion was so bad, it took several days to recover all 30 men. My father and brother were among the last found. The caskets were brought home, and later taken to the church for funeral services. We wanted so much to open them, to see them one last time. But we were not allowed to because of the terrible deterioration of the bodies.

My mother was never compensated for my father's and brother's deaths, not one red cent. People don't know how lucky they are today.

Player 3: Please, please, let's not focus on the negative. We're supposed to work together. Now would anyone like an autograph? No charge. You can take 'em for your kids.

W 1: My kids never have the famous superstars as role models. Daddy was and is our role model. My children have come to realize how dangerous their father's job was, and they respect him even more now for the risks that he took daily.

P 2: I could tell you a thing about risks, little lady. You try batting against Randy Johnson at twilight.

P 3: Again, I must ask everyone to not argue. Divisiveness is our enemy when we must realize management is the true enemy. Management is viciously trying to pad its pockets with our money. We must work together as one. Please, tell us how we can be of help to you.

M 3: Since so many of you are big names and have big incomes, we'd sure appreciate some contributions to our fund for...

P 3: Oh, a, uh, contribution, well, we'd love to but things are awfully tight now with the strike so recent and all, and we've already signed up for some charity. That's why we have to work overtime signing autographs. It's not big money, but it helps out. In fact, we have a signing now, fellas—$20 a pop. It's for that black liver or black tongue group.

10

BASEBALL'S FORGOTTEN MAN

Baseball is the best. But it's like everything else.
I guess, some players for you, some against you.
I'm a tough guy, gambler on horses, a slave driver
and in general a disgrace to the game. I wish
I knew why. I only wanted to win.
—Rogers Hornsby

I should have guessed that searching for Rogers Hornsby would be the equivalent of a bad hop to the balls. He was every manager's greatest pain (and when he was a manager, every player's and club president's), but like a double hot fudge brownie sundae to a diet-conscious model, he was too good to pass up. God, those statistics: a .400 average over five years, the triple crown in 1922, the .358 lifetime average. And he did that as a middle infielder, mainly at second base. Who cares if he couldn't go back on popups?

I should also have guessed Hornsby would give me trouble because he's given me trouble before. For years I've played one of those table-top baseball board games. Inevitably I would select Rogers as though he were my prodigal son. Inevitably he would disappoint me. He wouldn't hit righthanders or lefthanders, early innings or late, clutch situations or blowouts. I'd bench him, drop him in the order, berate him, extol him. Nothing worked. The season would end, Rogers' average would be in the .220s, we'd pick new teams, and the cycle would resume. I understand how battered wives stay with their husbands. The behavior is abhorrent but the potential for good—the charm, the smile, the body, the humor—is too great to ignore.

When I got my list of gravesites, I saw that Rogers was interred in Hornsby Bend, Texas. After checking several state maps and atlases, including the imposing *Rand McNally Marketing Guide*, the town's and cemetery's location remained unknown. For one of the few times, a State Information Center was helpful. A woman led me to the *Texas Handbook*, one of the Lone Star State's co-Bibles (the *NRA Handbook* is the other) and I read about Rueben Hornsby, Rogers' great-grandfather, who settled in what would become Travis County just outside of Austin. That's where I would find Hornsby Bend and the family cemetery.

I stared at the No Trespassing sign that blocked the dirt path to the Hornsby burial ground. Turning back was unthinkable. Unfortunately, I did think of being emasculated by zealous dogs, as well as being gunned down by rabid Texans. The state legislature had just passed a concealed gun law. As I hopped the fence, I pictured a good ol' boy unconcealing his piece and shoving it into my ribs with a flasher's delight.

A cardinal flew past me toward the cemetery. Under the circumstances, it was the best omen I could have hoped for. What if it had been the mascot from one of Rogers' other teams? A Cub I could have handled. A Red would have been interesting. Maybe Lenin or Trotsky or perhaps even Angela Davis. I don't know about a Brown, though. Paul? James? Ollie? A Giant or Brave would have sent me scurrying for cover.

My confidence grew as I walked. The PW pipe I carried would be at least partly effective against dogs. I didn't feel bad about the trespassing. I'm not a lawbreaker, really; I rarely do what I'm not supposed to. I floss, remember birthdays, and am punctual, so what's a little trespassing? Besides, I figured Rogers would have done the same. He was stubborn, doing what he wished, and saying what he thought. More than all his accomplishments, he said he was proudest of not being "a baseball hypocrite…I've never taken back anything I ever said and I've never failed to say exactly—and I mean exactly—what I was thinking. To everybody— from the owner to the ballboy."

Barbed fences lined each side of the path. About five minutes from the main road, I saw a historic marker. Rueben and Sarah Hornsby had built a home at the spot in 1832. Known for its "Christian hospitality," it was also the site where "Josiah Willbarger recovered after being scalped in 1833." I smoothed my hair and continued. The graveyard was another quarter-

mile down the path and was as forgotten as a long over-
due history assignment. The cardinal was back,
perched on the cemetery fence.

I squeezed between the gate and fence and began
reading headstones. There was a roster full of
Hornsbys: Ella and Exa, Harold and Maud, Bessie and
Jessie and James, Fred and Frank, and more. I
tramped through the brush, muttering that I had worn
shorts. Of course, I hadn't expected a trek through
Austin's rain forest. The slick undergrowth slid against
my shins and thighs and thick spiderwebs latched onto
my hair, face, arms, legs, and chest. And then I found
Rogers in a back corner. Grass and plants converged
upon his stone like angry fans. The spot was a solitary
one—and then the mosquitoes arrived.

My custom had been to take a photo and sketch the
gravesite. I snapped a picture and figured I'd leave
because of the mosquitoes. It'd be easy enough to draw
the marker from a snapshot. After a half-dozen bites I
got ready to leave. I looked at the headstone again and
decided not to. I would be as headstrong as the granite
it was made of and as stubborn as the man whose remains lay beneath it.

Hornsby Bend, TX   May 22, 1995

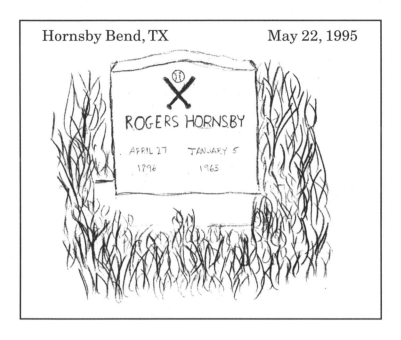

Drawing was difficult as swarming mosquitoes
sought to distract me from my task. How many such
annoyances do we have? Pesky non-entities obscuring
goals, keeping objectives at arm's length, our dreams
always for tomorrow. If anyone knew about setting his
eyes on a target, it was Rogers Hornsby. Actually, in
order to fulfill his goals he set them on little else. He
only read the headlines of newspapers and did not attend movies, fearing his batting eye would suffer.

The sketch was more hastily done than most, but
doing it was my tribute to Rogers' determination. It
was a tribute to mine as well. My efforts pleased me,
but I couldn't shake the loneliness of the place. Far off,
grown over, fenced in, tucked away. It wasn't right.

Two mornings later I sat at the Austin Public Library reading Rogers' 1963 obituary. When he jumped

to the Mexican League in the 1940s, most of his life had been spent in the majors as player, manager, or coach. A reporter asked why he had switched to an inferior, more anonymous brand of baseball.

"It's baseball, isn't it?" Rogers responded. "I don't know any other business and I don't want to. There's no place for me in the game here. Baseball has forgotten me."

Sadly, baseball had done so again.

11

TRIS SPEAKER AND THE NEW ANTIQUITY

But we really didn't discuss the whole question of segregation. It was something that existed and that we saw when we went to the town, into Troy, to the dimestore. We saw the sign saying White Only or Colored. When you went to go to the water fountain, you knew not to drink of that fountain that said White Only, that you were directed to drink out of the one saying Colored. You couldn't go to the soda fountain and get a Coke. Somehow we grew up knowing that you couldn't cross that line.
—John Lewis

Before the twister, the little town of Hubbard, Texas, thrived. Fourteen grocery stores, two theaters, even an opera. Saturdays bustled. Hubbard was, well, the area's hub and residents from neighboring towns walked the elevated sidewalks, visiting, shopping, flirting, gossiping. The routine was constant. Change was for the seasons and the pockets.

Tris Speaker spent his days there, too. He was a big part of the community, growing up outside of town, playing ball against neighboring teams, turning to ranching during the off-season, never acting better than his fellow residents, running errands with his boots on. Smiling, joking, laughing.

Hubbard is proud of Speaker and would like to honor him in some manner. His headstone is unassuming, there's hardly even a baseball reference. The owner of the local funeral home said he has tried for years to convince Speaker's niece and namesake, Tris Speaker Scot, to permit a larger memorial. The owner is a huge man and a huge baseball fan.

"Fenway, the street vendors, the park in the middle of the neighborhood. To me, that's baseball....I'm a traditionalist."

In more ways than one. Framed portraits of Robert E. Lee and Stonewall Jackson, two-thirds of the Southern trinity (Jefferson Davis is the other), hung somberly on the wall. I acknowledged them as I would a family picture.

"You almost have to have them around," he said, and then reminisced of days gone by. "In the 1960s our school flew the Confederate flag and played Dixie and the blacks loved it."

He paused, his first in a stream of conversation. He was wistful, thinking of the good ol' days of panty raids, boys will be boys and you could tell a good Dago joke, or hell, even a colored one simply because it was funny and not have to worry about the U.N. Security Council having a hissy fit and debating it at the next meeting and reading about it in all the newspapers because of those damn, bleeding-heart, liberal reporters.

"Some people compare the South to Nazi Germany," he said, "but I don't see that." (I did not ask how many funeral homes in Germany have neatly framed portraits of Rommel and Goering in the director's homey office.)

I returned to the antique shop I had stopped at when I arrived earlier that morning. A girl, a high school student, offered lunch. The $5.95 price was beyond my budget, but she and the owner had been helpful so I felt obligated to accept. Besides, I could think of no excuse. Four women were seated near me. Old, proper, educated, and well-dressed.

"What are race relations like here?" I asked.

Silence. One looked furtively about and leaned near. Softly: "Are there any colored here?"

Are there? Coloreds? Here? Yes, there are coloreds here. I'm colored. Black. One-eighth, which used to be enough to get you killed. My great-grandfather was black and his father was black, and he was a slave and I'm proud of that. My brother looks particularly black and he married a black woman. Is that enough color for you?

I looked around. "No."

Hours later I wished I had shared my thoughts. But to do so with these women—all kind, all proper, all ladylike—would be like disputing my grandmother. Also, I wondered how active of a role I should play in such situations. Should I observe and report or act and confront? I never resolved the conflict. I was caught in endless thinking, which is as worthwhile as not thinking at all.

Of course, there are some for whom thought is not a problem. The antique shop owner said she returned to Hubbard "to preserve a way of life" in a place that's been "dying on the vine since the '50s." There was order and direction to the town when it was a hub of activity, she said, but now the young leave as soon as they can. "Everyone came to Hubbard on Saturdays. You couldn't even get a parking place."

I asked if the blacks came to town. I'd seen several drive down the main avenue, shopping at the store, but where did they live? While biking through the wide, tree-lined streets, I'd seen no sign of them. They seemed like subterranean operatives, emerging for necessities, scurrying back for survival.

"They never ventured into town," said the shop owner. "They stayed on the other side of the tracks. Some of the greatest people I ever knew lived over there. They weren't like the blacks of today: 'Gimme, gimme, gimme. You owe me.' I don't owe nobody nothing, and neither does our government."

Again, I was taken aback. This was no beer-bellied, red-necked trucker with the St. Andrew's cross branded on his heart and rear window who spewed hatred. This was the genteel side of racism, a woman with whom I had sipped ice water hours before while swapping stories of Tris and her uncle. What do you say to the devil who has kind eyes and no horns? Again, I chose silence.

I excused myself. I needed to leave. I needed to flee this constrictive presence. I needed to see a black face.

It was lovely. His face. His old, beaten, wrinkled, knowing, beautiful black face. A blue fishing hat topped his 75-year-old head like a crown. The few teeth he had went off at crazy angles, and he spoke through chapped lips. His tired eyes had seen Speaker, Banks, and other greats play ball at the now overgrown park not far from the dirt road where we stood. This was the other side of the tracks.

"Is there still segregation here?"

"Oh, yes, this is the South."

"That's just the reality?"

"You don't have to worry about things happening like you used to but it's still segregation."

"Will it ever change?"

"I don't see how. I don't see how it can."

But he was familiar with seemingly lost causes. As a litter carrier in the medical corps in World War II, he taxied bodies and the remains of bodies during the brutal Battle of the Bulge. "I thought we were going to lose. I don't see how we didn't." We didn't, of course, and soon after that Jackie became a Dodger. (Older blacks invariably use the familiar first name when referring to Robinson.) A year later, in 1948, Larry Doby joined the Cleveland Indians, integrating the American League. Speaker was a coach on that team and became Doby's mentor.

"Tris made Larry Doby. Larry was a po' fielder, a good hitter but a po' fielder. Balls hit him on the shoulders, everywhere, but Tris kept working with him."

Indeed, Doby was poor. He led the league with 14 errors as a rookie in 1948 and had one of the worst fielding percentages. He improved some his second year and then became considerably better. I thought of Speaker and Doby, products of segregated Southern societies and separate generations, coming to the park early or staying late, working together. The aging white star and the promising young Negro. What did Speaker think of Doby? Did the familiar Cleveland arrow across the wool uniform's shirt help Speaker forget the blackness beneath? Or did it even matter? Did the Gray Eagle willingly take Doby under his aging wings? I was impressed that a white Southerner would show such interest in a black man. I would liked to have met him.

"I met him," said the man. "I was hitchhiking from Waco. Tris stopped an' asked where I was goin'. Said he was sorry he couldn't help me, he was on his way to Houston. He gave me a pencil." A pencil?

Tracks really do not exist in Hubbard, but there are barriers. Main Street dies into nothingness. The south end of town, including City Hall, was swept away by the tornado in 1973. Beyond it are the black neighborhoods.

There, the streets are mostly unpaved, the elementary school does not compare to the one on the other side of town, homes are in disrepair, and loose dogs are more effective than any Keep Out sign. There is enough junk in front of many homes to open an antique store. But you needn't enter any to see the past preserved.

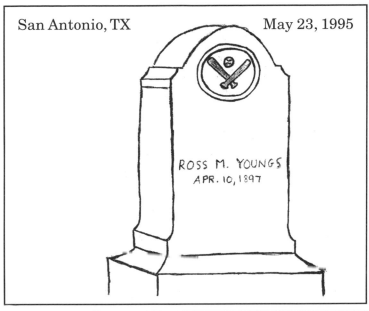

San Antonio, TX   May 23, 1995

ROSS M. YOUNGS
APR. 10, 1897

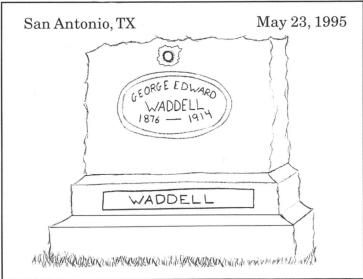

San Antonio, TX   May 23, 1995

GEORGE EDWARD
WADDELL
1876 — 1914

WADDELL

Seven Hall of Famers died before their 40th birthdays, including the two buried in San Antonio's Mission BurialPark: Ross Youngs, 30, and Rube Waddell, 37.

12

THE TURTLE'S LONG ROAD

Cowards die many times before their death;
The valiant never taste of death but once.
—William Shakespeare

Gee, they're big, ain't they?
—Lloyd Waner to brother Paul on the size of their opponents, the Yankees, in the 1927 World Series

The turtle was larger than a sheet of notebook paper. It was half-way across the road and now seemed uncertain which way to go. I knew where I wanted to go—Little Rock, which was only 136 miles away from the rest area I had spent the night at, but I was making little progress. I was spreading myself thin and needed to focus so I pulled off the road and watched the turtle.

Each town I came to was worthy of a stop, but if I stopped at every worthy place, I'd still be traveling when Chelsea Clinton graduated from college. Of course, I had to visit Hope, her daddy's hometown. The president's childhood home was as exciting as his vice president and as stimulating as the national budget. I found no local restaurant downtown, probably because of the nearby fast food franchises off the highway. I bought a cake doughnut for 27 cents at a bakery to boost the local economy. It appeared in need.

The turtle was also making little progress. Like me, it was floundering. We both had far to travel, though his status was far more precarious than mine in this state where motorists run over turtles for sport. For a greater challenge, I suppose locals could drive on yellow divider lines. I snapped a photo and returned to Nellie with renewed focus. For the rest of the trip and beyond, I felt guilty for not saving the hapless creature from crazed Razorbacks in speeding white Broncos.

A woman, whose voice was stuck on high, and her husband munched on sandwiches in the office of Little Rock's Roselawn Cemetery. They noticed my bike and were horrified when I told them I had ridden the several miles from Little Rock University.

Him: "You don't have any bullet holes?"

Her (repeatedly): "YOU'RE BRAVE. YOU NEED TO BE CAREFUL."

Him: "There've been a number of shootings in the area."

It used to be a good area, explained the man, an Arkansas highway patrolman, but gangs have overtaken it. Residents have either moved or stay inside, prisoners in their homes, locking out evil, locking in fear.

Bill Dickey is buried in Roselawn. The family stone features his team's familiar insignia—a top hat on the backdrop of a baseball with Yankees blaring across it. Dickey was the leader of teams which for years showed no fear. They knew they would win and they did. (Dickey played in eight World Series in his 17 years, winning seven of them, three in sweeps). Their confidence and swagger only increased the opposition's fright. Fear is the gift of one's life to another. It freezes and paralyzes and makes even simple tasks as daunting as the turtle's attempt to cross the road.

After sketching Dickey's grave I asked the couple for directions to Central High School, where nine black students risked their lives to integrate an all-white school in 1957. It's real close, they said, but please don't go. IT'S DANGEROUS. I wasn't concerned. It was daylight and there'd been no problems in biking to Roselawn.

A block from the campus, three boys walked toward me. They were probably middle school students. They were loud and boisterous. And black. Typically, I stare at people I approach, hoping for eye contact and an exchange of greetings and even smiles. I looked toward them and quickly turned away. They might consider my actions a challenge, and who knows what could happen then.

My gaze shifted to the reeling dark street below. The constricted breath, the tightened grip, the jellied legs. I was scared but only momentarily for the fear had turned to guilt within a few pedal strokes. We've been conditioned to fear the urban black male. I teach a number of such students and many have shared how pedestrians cross the street or tense up or hold a purse or bag a little tighter when they walk past. Most share their stories with anger or frustration or sadness or, more often, all three. Others say they don't care, it doesn't matter. The latter students give themselves away. They have yet to perfect stoicism as a protective shell.

What kind of shells did the Central High Nine develop? Their integration battle is preserved in movies and newsreels. The footage is surreal. The students, known as Negroes then, dare not look around during their first days at the majestic, yellow-bricked Central High. Their eyes are focused ahead or down. Still, they cannot help but see the snarling mob and stone-faced, unhelpful National Guard.

One girl, Elizabeth Eckford, dressed prettily in a black and white dress she made for her first day of

school, is apart from her group. She neither knows
where to look nor where to go. She looks everywhere
for help and goes nowhere. She is bewildered, a small
animal surrounded by wolves. The comments are not
audible on the newsreels but sneering faces of hate
have their own voices.

An angel appears. A white woman steps from the
crowd. If she is scared, she does not show it. She guides
the girl to a bus and helps her on. She broke her
society's code and chipped away at its segregated back.

Thirty-eight years later, an assistant principal reluctantly gave me a tour of the school, which is 40 percent white and 60 percent black. (The faculty,
meanwhile, is 70 percent white.) The gymnasium was
being reconstructed after arson caused $500,000 in
damage. From a second-floor window the assistant
principal and I looked upon a patio built by parents
because students complained there were too few places
to eat lunch on campus. About 35 students chatted and
ate in small groups. None were integrated.

Still on my bike and still in areas I was told to
avoid, I made my way toward the capitol. It sits on the
site of a former prison, an apt location with that
summer's forthcoming indictment of Gov. Jim Tucker.
En route, I saw a small cafeteria named Yancy's. I
sensed the food would meet my holy trinity of cuisine:
cheap, tasty, and abundant. I was hungry but hesitant
to enter. It was clearly a black restaurant and I questioned how I would be welcomed. Appetite being the
better part of valor, I walked in.

Conversation stopped and diners sat motionless like portraits in haunted houses where only the eyes move. I grabbed a tray and headed self-consciously to the line. The server mumbled something. Her glare made me so uneasy that I didn't ask for a clarification. I pointed at the food I recognized: blackeyed peas, okra, corn muffins, and peach cobbler.

The cashier smiled. It was a gap-toothed, twisted-toothed, missing toothed smile that no orthodontist should ever consider touching. It put me at ease better than any lock or weapon or sermon or song. It made everything right, if not in the big, cold world, then at least in this small, warm cafeteria. I sat confidently and contentedly. It was the best meal of the trip.

And I had nearly passed it by. My presence was no longer overtly offensive to other customers. Fear attacks the senses and emotions first, obscuring and distorting reality. I sat at my table and listened to laughter and conversation. I knew I had exaggerated the reaction to my entrance. There was no doubt disapproval from some, but my fear had heightened it. My shell protected me, but also kept me from seeing what was really there.

Fear is the freest of gifts, ours for the taking. According to legend, the Pirates took it during batting practice before Game 1 of the 1927 World Series. The Yankees' Murderers Row bashed homer after homer as Pittsburgh looked meekly on. The Pirates promptly played like turtles much of the time, rolled onto their shells, and got baked four straight. I don't condemn them, though. I am a turtle much of the time, fearfully pulling in head and limbs at the first sign of danger.

You can imagine other turtles, real ones, in the growth alongside Route 67 in Arkansas, stretching their heads from the grass as they consider the road before them. That they want to cross it there is no doubt. Many try, carrying as much protection as they can. Their quest is foolish, their journey pointless. But the wiser ones know there is wisdom through experience and experience is earned only by leaving the comfortable, where fear is a magnet.

The first steps are shaky. Blurs of danger speed past. Already committed, there is no turning back. Many will never make it, but they have to try.

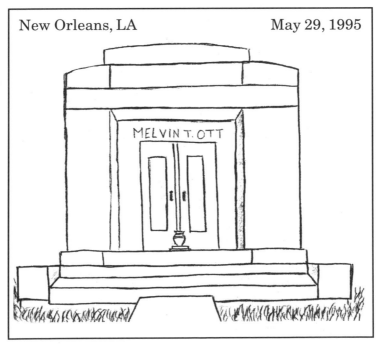

New Orleans, LA   May 29, 1995

The dead in New Orleans' cemeteries are interred above ground because of the high water table. Mel Ott's crypt is large but, unlike others in Metarie Cemetery, is not ornate.

13

EDUCATION
MISSISSIPPI-STYLE

*It is only when we forget all our learning
that we begin to know.*
—Henry David Thoreau

*It don't make no difference how you say it,
just say it in a way that makes sense.
Did you ever meet anybody in your life
who didn't know what ain't means?*
—Dizzy Dean

I arrived in Wiggins, Mississippi, early morning of June 1. Dizzy Dean, the stranger than fiction, larger than life (at nearly 300 pounds after his retirement he was larger than most everything) pitcher for the Cardinals and Cubs retired in Wiggins. The most auspicious of players is buried inauspiciously with his

wife, Patricia Nash, in a tiny graveyard in neighboring
Bond, a town nearly forgotten.

Although Diz had been dead since 1974, he was
still well remembered. His home was now a Baptist
residence for troubled youths, and locals recalled him
fondly. "He was a liar," said a friend. "I'd constantly
have to tell that bastard off." Only in the South would
liar and bastard be complimentary. Southerners are
particular about their language, and sensitive. Their
words have as much grease as their food and is just as
delicious. Sentences slide in lyrical free verse.

Said one man of Dizzy, who caused a nationwide
grammar furor in 1946: "He was talking to the people
of the South. The South built baseball. He talked the
way they talked, the people of the South."

Well, apparently not the way everyone in the South
talked. A group of Missouri English teachers complained to the Federal Communications Commission
that Dizzy's treatment of the English language was
detrimental to students. They wanted him yanked

from the air because of such Deanisms as, "The runner just slud inter third safely, but he was awmost throwed out, the lucky stiff," "Just look how calmly and confidentially the batter is standing up down there next to the plate," and his use of "swanged" and "swunged."

The Saturday Review defended him: "Abuse of English is the standard occupational disease of the national pastime, a disease which, if cured, would do irreparable damage to the patient."

Diz came (camed? comed?) to his own defense in an article he wrote for United Press. "My mother died when I was three years old," he began, "and me and Paul had to go out and pick cotton to get dough to keep the fire up.

"I guess we didn't get much education.

"And I reckon that's why that now I come up with an ain't once in a while, and have the Missouri teachers all stirred up. They don't like it because I say that Marty Marion or Vern Stephens slud into second base. What do they want me to say—slidded?"

Dizzy-1, English Teachers-0.

I walked into the Stone County Courthouse in Wiggins, hoping a trial was in progress. It was Friday, though, the court's day off. I went to the top floor and opened a door to a balcony. The sight startled me. Black men and women sat as if in mourning, waving cheap dimestore fans, futile against the heat. They sweated and looked toward the courtroom below.

The black man at the defense table did not move. Attorneys, court workers, jurors, and the judge chatted idly as if they had a few moments to spare before the main attraction began.

The figures vanished and spirits swirled in a dizzying storm. I had to remind myself to breathe. I felt the generations who had sat there, suffocating from heat and injustice, fanning, always fanning, praying for a break from their skin-induced punishment.

I told the custodian, a gold-toothed, black man named Maxie, about my vision.

"They brought us down from the balcony," he chuckled. "If they gonna hang the boy, they got to have the momma close to see her cry."

His laugh was an act. Humor as a cover. It's advantageous at times to appear the fool or the comedian. But as we talked the cover evaporated, the jokes stopped. He spoke of Emmit Till's murder and how he later took his four sons to the scene "to make 'em aware. Not to make 'em radicals. To make 'em aware."

To make 'em aware of the system and how it operates. I was more curious with how individuals operated within it. For weeks I had tried to put myself in the place of blacks and whites, those who are 50 or older, those who remember what it used to be like—and don't be fooled, it used to be much worse. When in restaurants and banks and post offices and grocery stores I looked for some betrayal of their feelings. Thirty years ago—no, less than that—these black men and women were subservient, prejudged, condemned. Now they walk in the same doors, stand in the same lines, use the same fountains, order at the same counters, even sit on the same toilet seats. There must be whites— perhaps the benevolent-looking grandfather over

there, the one whose fingers tremble as he holds his
burger—who once held shut the doors to integration.
Who did he shut out? Was it another grandfather? Perhaps the man with the splotchy beard filled with white
who shuffles from the counter and sits in the booth
next to him. What do they feel? What do they remember? Can they forget? Should they forget? How do they
live together?

Maxie pondered the last question. We were on the
courthouse steps. Nearby, six inmates (five blacks and
one white) washed a police car.

"See that boy there," Maxie said, pointing to a
white child of 9 or 10. "If he'd a grown up with me, he'd
know how to run an' jump an' he'd eat my food. But he
goes home to his Daddy, who puts his chew in an' says,
'That's a nigger.' But then he goes to school an' his boy
meets my boy. 'My Daddy says you're a nigger.' And my
boy says, 'See those two eyeholes of yours? Well, I'm
going to cave them in if you say that.' And so now that
boy is confused and he learns you don't say that in
public....But that's OK because it's getting better. I
want you to know that. It's getting better. And it will
continue to get better because we've got the vote."

But aren't you angry? Or bitter?

"No, no, because they acted out of ignorance."

Throughout the region, I met blacks who echoed
the message. The whites did not know better. This level
of grace was beyond me, and I believed it was only possible because the movement was based on God and love
and courage. Finally, I began to understand. Thanks to
an aging custodian who didn't always speak proper
and could have hobnobbed right fine with Ol' Diz, my
ignorance was beginning to slud clean out of sight.

14

A HOLIDAY IN(N) ALABAMA

We couldn't hardly get a man in business to lead out in the fight (for civil rights in Birmingham), because he knew that his business was gone when he identified himself with the struggle. So we had to get a man that couldn't lose nothing but his life, and we found Fred Shuttlesworth.
—Ed Gardner

On the way from around the back of the house, this Klans—this policeman who was a Klansman— said to me… "If I was you I'd get outa town as quick as I could." I said, "Well, you tell them that I'm not going out of town…If God could save me through this, then I'm gon' stay here and clear up this," I said. "I wasn't saved to run…"
—Rev. Fred Shuttlesworth
after his home was bombed

Alabama was to have done nothing more than bridge Dizzy Dean's Mississippi and Ty Cobb's Georgia. (Is the South loaded with characters or what?) I had no plans to stop there and certainly did not intend to urinate on the steps of the state capitol in Montgomery.

But Joe Sewell, who replaced Ray Chapman as the Cleveland shortstop in 1920 when Chapman was killed by a Carl Mays' pitch, was an Alabaman. Sewell was one of a handful of Hall-of-Famers whose burial site was unknown to Cooperstown. He was born in Titus, a town on life support about 20 miles from Montgomery. Its three grocery stores had dwindled to one, and even that was closed on the early Friday afternoon I visited. Abandoned, rotting shacks interrupted the green. Only a small post office looked new. Everything else was lifeless, from the freshly cut lawns to the old, silent Baptist church and adjacent cemetery.

There was no town to speak of, only a scattering of homes, and they were not inviting. Sealed doors and drawn shades kept out heat and strangers. I suspected neither was welcome.

I knocked at the door of a house near the post office. An old woman answered and listened patiently.

"I don't know where he's buried," she said, "but my friend may. She's related to him." She let me in and hollered. "Say, this fella's a teacher from California and he's looking for Joe Sewell's grave. Do you know where he's buried?"

A pause. And then, from another room: "Joe? He's dead?"

A few phone calls and glasses of ice water later put

me at the lakeside home of Wilbur Hardin, a one-time
semi-pro catcher. "Joe's in Tuscaloosa, but I don't know
where." This made sense. Sewell graduated from Alabama and later coached there. Cemetery hunting
would not be productive until Monday, so I opted to
spend the weekend in Birmingham for a Barons game
and more of the Civil Rights atmosphere.

    During my pre-trip planning, I figured I would

spend my nights in campgrounds or youth hostels or exploit the invitations of friends, the ones who live hundreds or thousands of miles away and said at some point, "Come visit, we'd love you to visit." My hosts were unfailingly generous, but their free air-conditioned comfort spoiled me. The idea of paying for even rudimentary lodging was increasingly painful.

When I arrived in Birmingham on June 4, I had slept in Nellie five nights in a row. During that time, I perfected a sleeping system that I was as proud of as Steinbeck was of his washing machine mechanism. After two dismal nights in the front seat, I tried the back, laying my sleeping bag across it. I moved the front seat forward and inclined its back until it touched the steering wheel. I slept in one of two positions: either on my back with knees bent or on my right side with legs angled and the feet set on the driver's arm rest as though that were its sole purpose.

The accommodations were more comfortable than the floor I usually slept on at home. The backseat bed became a major part of the trip, providing reasonable comfort and saving money. I spent only $162 on lodging over five months on the road because of friends and the 48 nights in Nellie, including nine in a row in Ohio, Kentucky, and Indiana that left me delirious when I reached Chicago.

For safety reasons, I avoided sleeping on backroads. Hotel lots seemed reasonable. I usually arrived late and left early. Then, I discovered the benefits of the Holiday Inn in Hoover on the fringe of Birmingham, known as Bombingham in the 1960s, but now trying desperately to change its image.

I was certainly pleased by the hospitality. Crisp
apples at the front counter and cool tuna croissants in
the lobby. I also had access to the bathrooms, swimming pool, hot tub, and complimentary copies of *USA
Today*. Stationary and towels were even provided. The
pool was the real bonus and the Jacuzzi the exclama-
tion point. I hadn't bathed in days. I jumped into the
pool, subtly pulled a bar of Ivory from my trunks, submerged to the bottom, and soaped up. I popped up for
air and repeated the process, hoping the chlorine
would exterminate whatever pesky microscopic organ-
isms were partying in, over, and around my pores. The
hot tub was wonderful. As the heat swirled about, I
closed my eyes, leaned back, and...and was jarred by
my first loneliness of the trip.

I felt far away from loved ones. Heck, I was far
away from loved ones. My days were so packed with
activity that I rarely had time to dwell on being alone,
but the evenings were occasionally different. I wished
for company. First, a pair of high school sophomores,
boyfriend and girlfriend, hopped into the tub. The girl
had legs to Louisiana and serpentined them around
her ready to explode beau. Then, newlyweds who ignored my efforts of conversation. Finally, a South
Carolina couple with the unlikely names of Riley and
Page. They were a physically beautiful couple, and as
friendly as their names were aristocratic. We chatted
about Christopher Reeve's recent fall, our jobs, home.
Nothing important, except that it was terribly important to me. In striving for an ascetic life, I had effec-
tively convinced myself that people were just another
thing I could do without. They were nice to have

around, but so were smoked clams. And like the clams, I viewed them as more luxury than necessity. I prided myself on my solitude, on my ability to be alone, but I woke up one day and realized no one was there to acknowledge it.

I thought of Page and Riley often, appreciative of the randomness of events that soothed my loneliness on a June night. I began the trip with the belief that most people are good, that the country is populated with dear friends I had simply yet to meet. They were among the first.

After my weekend in Hoover, I drove to Tuscaloosa and saw the South's other side. Lumber trucks regularly threatened my and Nellie's existence on anorexic two-lane roads. The Confederate flag was emblazoned on a number of the trucks' radiator grills. Seeing the Stars and Bars zooming toward me at 60 miles per hour was as soothing as encountering a high voltage flashlight in the middle of the night.

I never got used to seeing the flag and I especially never got used to the language. When I arrived at Tuscaloosa Memorial Park, I chatted with an office worker about Sewell. The conversation (as all conversations seem to do in Alabama) turned to college football. The Crimson Tide was under NCAA investigation. "We gave the poor nigger an education," said the man, "he can't make it in the real world and says we paid him to play ball."

I ended the conversation abruptly and headed to Montgomery. The Civil Rights Memorial was there,

and I'd heard it was powerful. It was only a short distance from the capitol and directly in front of the
Southern Poverty Law Center, an advocacy group
whose curriculum material on tolerance and prejudice
I receive. The Memorial was to me what the Vietnam
Wall must be to vets. Water streamed down a black
granite facade. It also flowed down an upside down
cone, which had the names of martyred civil rights
workers engraved on top. My heroes. Our Christs.

Two security guards surveyed the scene. There'd
been bomb threats against the center, and they served
as protection.

I touched the wall and felt the cool streams against
my hand. The water did not soften my anger over the
need for guards. I left, first to see King's church, from
where he led the 1955 Bus Boycott. It is a small, red
brick building and stands as near to the formidable
white marble capitol as David did to Goliath.

The current capitol was completed in 1851, and 10
years later Jefferson Davis was inaugurated as president of the Confederacy on its then wooden steps. Stat-
ues of Davis are abundant throughout the South. It
wasn't quite six, darkness was still 90 minutes away,
and the capitol was silent, shut down like a ghost town.
The Alabama Flame of Freedom was out. The wind was
strong but it couldn't have extinguished the flame.
Maybe the blasphemy of such a flame in such a state
with such a past was responsible.

Or maybe it was the ghosts of the millions who
lived and died there. I thought of the slaves and of Rosa
Parks. I thought of Hank Aaron and Willie Mays and
Willie McCovey. I thought of my recent days in the

South: the Wiggins courthouse, Maxie, the casual use of "nigger," and the insensitivity if not hatred behind the Confederate flag. I thought of Hubbard, Texas. I thought of the bomb threats.

The foulness within me surged to get out. I'd taken my vitamins late that afternoon, so I was startled by the yellow fluorescence of my urine splashing on the white marble steps. The puddle grew along with my concern of being discovered. My contempt for the legacy of this place flowed down the steps that Jefferson Davis, George Wallace, and a host of others once walked up.

I returned to the memorial for a last look and to copy King's brief message engraved on the wall:

Until justice rolls down like waters
And righteousness like a mighty stream.

15

THE GOOD DIED YOUNG

...caressing each moment as an emerald
on temporary consignment...
—Alan Lightman

Doggedly, I searched for the Big Cat. It was like looking for that J.D. Salinger book among hundreds of Danielle Steele novels and *Reader's Digest* abridged editions. I maneuvered my way among the flatstones like Crazy Legs Hirsch, searching for the compact name whose size was so out of proportion to the man's bluntness and strength.

It was Saturday, June 17, and I had anticipated that the Yonah View Memory Gardens office in Demorest, Georgia, would be closed. I did not anticipate Yonah View's size. Known for lumbering and pretty Piedmont College, Demorest is a town of 1,300 situated less than two hours northeast of Atlanta. I figured the cemetery would also be small, so I could walk it and find Johnny Mize's grave without much trouble. I was eager to get to

Ty Cobb's grave in Royston, only 50 miles away, by the following day, Father's Day.

A couple landscaped their child's plot. Perhaps they would know where Mize lay and save me two or more hours of walking in the murky humidity. They didn't. I hoped his grave would stand out, but that was impossible for Yonah's markers are set supine, as protrusive as cardboard flaps on grass. If they had been headstones, I could have scanned a dozen or more in a few seconds.

I was in a hurry and felt badly for dismissing scores of dead. I felt I should pay greater acknowledgement and deeper respect. I scanned each marker, ignoring inscriptions and dates of birth and death, only checking the name, moving on, never stopping.

Never stopping until I came upon Leigh Bush and Julie Ann Harris. I can't say what stopped me. The wooden sunflowers? The motionless pinwheels? The flowers and birthday balloons? The small plaster angel, hands clasped in prayer, holding a plastic dolphin and small bracelet? Or the shiny bronze plaques which united the young women? They were born a month apart in 1975 and died within hours of each other in October 1993.

Each plaque contained a cross, an angel, and a pony-tailed basketball player shooting a two-footer. Their plaques also showed they were religious and sentimental and loving.

A LIFE LIVED WITH SO MUCH LOVE
WILL NEVER BE FORGOTTEN
BUT GOES ON FOREVER IN THE HEARTS
OF THOSE WHO REMEMBER.

and
TO ALL MY FRIENDS—I MISS YOU SO
BUT WHERE I AM YOU LIVE TO GO
A THOUSAND YEARS OR A LITTLE WHILE
LOOK FOR ME YOU'LL KNOW MY SMILE.

There were Bible verses from Phillipians and Prov-
erbs and a final message of love, one that was engraved
on a granite base. It was sandwiched between the girls'
basketball numbers, Leigh's 5 and Julie's 22:
"FRIENDS ARE FRIENDS FOREVER."

Probably a car crash. Briefly, I acknowledged the
tragedy. I'm sure they were good kids, the kind with
hope and smiles and enthusiasm who make teaching
the world's easiest and most rewarding of jobs. I tried
to shake my sadness. I still needed to locate Mize, who
I found nearby. His bronze plaque also had the shining
appearance of the not too long dead. It had the obliga-
tory birth and death information, but then had the look
of a page from a stat book.

It also had the look of someone who was bragging.
Less than one-third of the graves I saw had baseball
references, and nearly all of those were tastefully done,
usually some mention of the Hall of Fame. Even Ruth's
colossal stone was laced with humility. It seemed that
Mize wasn't aware there was more to life than baseball.

I returned to Leigh and Julie. Though not nearly as
famous as Demorest's most reknowned citizen, their
perspective on life was clear. Basketball was obviously
a part of their lives, probably a major part. But on their
markers, basketball was only the backdrop for the
ocean and flowers and friends and love. Something

about their lives drew me to them. Amputees talk of phantom pain, of maintaining feeling where their limbs once were. Is it any more odd to think that the love these girls shared was present beyond the grave and it was their love I felt on an empty Georgia afternoon?

Two weeks later I returned to Demorest, still pulled by the girls. I was anxious for more information. With the help of a librarian named Ruth, who said she was named after the Babe, I found the telling copy of *The Northeast Georgian*. The accident was the lead story. Leigh and Julie were passengers in a 1980 Jeep Renegade on Saturday, October 9, 1993. The vehicle went off the road when rounding a curve, skidded 132 feet, hit a ditch, and flew 48 feet through the air into the path of a Ford wagon. A month into their freshman year at Piedmont, they were preparing for their first college game.

"They couldn't wait," said their high school basketball coach, Sammy Cunningham. "They wanted me to come see their dorm room. They said they had decorated it really nice. They always wanted to go somewhere together. Leigh had offers to play at Clemson and other schools as well. She always asked what they could offer to Julie. If Julie wasn't part of the package, Leigh wasn't interested. They walked every aspect of their lives together and they went together."

And when they went, according to a cemetery worker, it seemed that most of the town came to see them off, many more than had attended Mize's farewell only three months earlier.

16

FATHER'S DAY WITH TY COBB

*It wasn't that I gave baseball a second thought
as a career. My overwhelming need was to prove
myself a real man. Playing ball there was a
chance to become more than another schoolboy
and the son of Professor Cobb.*
—Ty Cobb

It was perversely appropriate to spend Father's
Day in Royston, Georgia, with Ty Cobb. Educated, brilliant, demanding, stern, William Herschel Cobb, Ty's
father, was a community leader in this northern
Georgia town of rolling hills. When 17-year-old Tyrus
left home to play professional ball, the father's final
words were clear: "Don't come home a failure."

Ty didn't have a chance to fail for he returned only
three weeks later. His father was dead, shot by Ty's

mother. She thought he was a prowler, she told authorities. Some say she was having an affair.

1981: My senior year of college. I was in the dorm hallway with several friends, doing nothing more elevating than trading insults. A door opened and a freshman and his dad appeared. A parent visit. No big deal, but we still respectfully stopped our banter for a moment.

"Bye, Dad, I love you."

"I love you, Scott."

They embraced and Scott kissed Dad on the cheek. Farewell. Scott returned to his room. Witnesses to this most impossible of acts, we sat stunned. The awkward silence remains with me. Senseless conversation no longer had a purpose; it was no longer funny. We left the hall noiselessly, entering empty rooms of unspoken affection with our fathers. I don't think it's unrealistic to believe that any one of us would have preferred a kiss from Dad to the woman of our dreams.

Sadly, most men have not progressed far from the fifth-grade boy who showed affection with a punch to the shoulder or a well-turned putdown. I have male friends who I greet with a handshake, though I desire to embrace. To some men I cannot close letters with words of love and I certainly cannot say, "I love you."

Until 1992 I had never told my father I loved him. Maybe in a card I did, but that's cheating, like serving imitation lobster. I feared he would die, suddenly, unexpectedly, before I could say that short, trite, overused, life-altering, world-changing, most powerful of phrases. I love you. Two pronouns and a verb, for God's sake, and I couldn't do it.

Neither could Dad. Oh, he showed it in a thousand ways, striving to make up in action what he could not express in words. His silence justified my own, I thought. But at age 31 I could no longer wait. I have swarming visions of loved ones dead. Death hovers above friends and I wonder who will go first. I shake my head, squeeze my eyes shut, and try to block the inevitable. The funeral: Dad—dead, silent. Me—breathless, speechless, unable to cry, suffocating on the words I never said. I love you, Dad. You know that's right. You know that. My omission is an unforgiving one.

I speak. Finally. At Black Angus. A restaurant made holy by love. We talk. Actually, he talks. About marrying Mom and getting her three sons in the bargain. About the responsibility of taking on a family.

"That must have been hard," I said. I have shared that before, but this time I continued. "I appreciate what you've done and I want you to know I love you."

It was like sex for the first time. Huge buildup, worry, tension, how do I do it, what will she think. And then. It's over. Oh, so that's what it's like. Thank God, it's over.

I was relieved, but I wasn't sure Dad had heard. He continued on his prime rib and we with our conversation. But I said what I needed. Cobb never had the chance. How much of his genius was from his own mother shooting his own father? The .367 average, the 4,191 hits, the 2,245 runs, the 892 stolen bases, the anger, the ferocity, how much of that was proof that he was not a failure?

You can see him tearing around the bases, spiking the third baseman as he slides in with a triple. He gets up, wipes the infield from his mouth, and subtly looks toward the stands. "How was that, Dad?"

But Dad never answers.

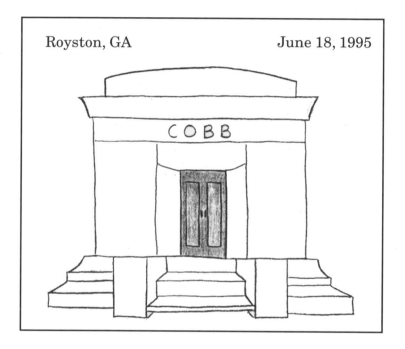

Royston, GA   June 18, 1995

17

TRAVEL HELL
IN FLORIDA

I'm glad it's over. Before anything else,
understand that I am glad it's over.
—Ted Williams

I picked up a brochure for the Ted Williams Hitters
Hall of Fame at the Welcome Center when I entered
Florida. Teddy Ballgame's Museum would be a fitting
final stop to the Sunshine State. With Lajoie, Terry,
Billy Herman, Ray Dandridge, Jimmy Foxx, and Paul
Waner, Florida boasted a collection of hitters second
only to New York's lineup: Ruth, Gehrig, Frisch,
Brouthers, Jackie Robinson, Keeler, and Duffy. Even
dead, they'd rival today's Mets.

Florida and New York are also two of seven states
with more than 10 deceased Hall-of-Famers. Illinois,
Ohio, Massachusetts, Pennsylvania, and California are
the others (notice the definite leaning toward sunshine

and the Northeast). My goal was to visit Florida's 12 graves in three days. It was a foolish idea, like foregoing a relaxing week on the Gulf coast for 30 minutes in one of the state's ubiquitous tanning salons.

There are consequences in hurrying, whether it's getting a quick tan or trying to breeze along the perimeter of one of the nation's longest state coastlines. On my first day in Florida, I toured a plantation and then stopped in St. Augustine. After all, it is America's oldest city and I am a history teacher; I stayed only briefly. I was tired and frustrated. I was trying to do and see too much. As a result, I didn't see much of anything but the preponderance of overpriced restaurants and underdressed women, each creating its own particular agony. By the time I reached Cedar Hill Cemetery in Daytona Beach, I had driven 260 miles and felt that the trip's focus was slipping as it had done in Arkansas. I needed to slow down but didn't think I could.

"If there was a Hall-of-Famer here, I'd know it," a Cedar Hill administrator told me. He sent me to the office across the street. An old woman was at the counter. Just give me the information, I thought, as I was in too much of a hurry to chat. She was 79, I learned, and was as sturdy as a pillow. She was not the oldest person I'd seen, but her fingers looked it. She squinted at the map in search of Nap Lajoie's lot number. My impatience grew until I looked at her fingers again. The skin was piled loosely and high, their elasticity probably gone for years. It seemed that she possessed enough skin for another 10 fingers. They were lovely. Their beauty was not the airbrushed perfection of a model's cheek. Rather it was the natural beauty of a field's furrow or the creases in bark. My grandmother must have fingers like them, but I had never noticed. I fought the urge to touch this woman's fingers; that would be impossibly rude. How sad we cannot burst into a stranger's life.

Still squinting, even with a magnifying glass, she struggled with the map.

"The doctor says I have old eyes."

"Really."

"Anyone would have old eyes, if they had to bury three family members in a year. My husband was bad enough, but when you have to bury your child, there's nothing worse. I didn't think I could go on. He died in San Francisco. I couldn't go out there. His friends called and told me not to. They said I wouldn't recognize him."

AIDS. He must've died of AIDS. I didn't ask. I didn't need to.

"He had a brain tumor and just wasted away."

My shirt felt blasphemous. It was olive green with National Brain Tumor Foundation written on the front and back. I'd gotten it because it was unique and sure to draw attention. Six weeks earlier, at Zion National Park in Utah, a woman asked if I worked for the foundation. "Oh, yes," I said, "I'm a brain surgeon." Harmless self-amusement. My new vocation was enjoyable until the woman divulged her past as an X-ray technician and asked how radiation technology had changed in the last several years. I fled from the topic idiotically and now, with this heartbroken woman, I felt as if my shirt mocked her loss. I felt terrible. She's burying family while I hip-hop around the country.

I crossed the street once more, and the administrator, a balding man named John, helped me search for Lajoie's grave. He was a Yankee fan since baseball's Golden Age—the 1950s. Musial, Moose, Mickey, Whitey, Williams, Willie, Yogi.

Dirt and mold cover Napoleon Lajoie's stone in Daytona Beach, Florida.

"Two out in the ninth," he said, "Yogi's coming up, game on the line, you just knew he was going to come through. The greatest clutch hitter by far."

He needed no prompting to continue his display of nostalgia or to voice his fury. Like scores of people I met across the nation, he was angry at baseball. To them, to me, baseball had changed. Today's game is as close to yesterday's as fast food is to Mom's cooking.

"The downfall began with the coke mess (in the late-'70s)," John explained. "Now the Yankees have

Steve Howe, a seven-time offender. They have Darryl Strawberry, a two-time offender. What is this telling the kids? That it's OK to do drugs?"

Stabbings from below drew my attention from his tirade. I looked to see my feet covered with ants. Fire ants. They charged into my flesh. Unimposing in appearance, they were tenacious and came with big, powerful jaws. If Leo Durocher or Billy Martin were ants, they'd be fire ants. John spoke on, glancing toward my feet once but otherwise indifferent to my anguish and casual attempts to brush them off. In a CPR class some months before, a fireman told me that many choking victims are found dead in restaurant bathrooms because they don't want to make a scene at the table. At the time I thought such behavior foolish, yet I was now choosing to not flail wildly at carnivorous insects because I was concerned with my image in front of a bald guy I'd just met who berated baseball amidst a bunch of dead people who presumably had other concerns. It was June 21, the first day of summer, and I felt eminently vincible.

When I reached Miami Beach two days later, my feet had new terrain. Two dozen mini volcanoes covered them, oozing a milky liquid. Thunderstorms added to my misery. They were violent and wet but did nothing to deter the humidity. When driving, I had two forgettable options: drive with windows down, easing the humidity but letting the pounding heavens in, or with windows up, turning the car into an unwanted sauna.

Exhausted, I checked into a youth hostel, sharing my room with a gregarious Australian. He had just returned from a year in Bolivia and was a fan of American pop culture. He too was oblivious to my agony, this time my need for sleep. Finally, I explained I had to rest. The next morning was already uncomfortably humid at 7:30. I approached Nellie nervously because I had neglected to put her in a garage. It appeared nothing had been disturbed until I put my key into emptiness. The driver's door lock was gone, popped out with a rod, probably while I answered questions about pet rocks and the Beatles.

The vandal was apparently no thief. The bike rack was there, and so were the stove and tent and a box with miscellaneous papers and nearly $2,000 in traveler's checks. It seemed as though I had nothing of interest to the vandal, and then I noticed my blue bag was gone. It was filled with assorted baseball items— the *Bill James Historical Baseball Abstract*, the *First Fireside Book of Baseball*, *A Donald Honig Reader*, an autographed photo of Vada Pinson a student gave me as a farewell gift, and, most painfully, a spiral notebook containing hours of research and pages of information. Perhaps the culprit was a crazed sabermetrician.

Depressed and tired, I still had to see Jimmy Foxx's and Bill Klem's graves in Miami and Ed Walsh's in Pompano Beach. It was late once I had finished and began cutting across the state on Highway 41 en route to Sarasota. On a number of occasions, I pulled off the road and turned the engine off. The silence was medicinal, and a welcome break from the plague of frogs which hopped to their death into my radiator grill. At least the frogs' demise was eventful. Mine was fading into a mass of sweat and sleeplessness.

Two nights at a hostel in Clearwater helped revive me. I spent much of the time talking to a mailman on vacation from Scotland. He visits the U.S. whenever he can and had an expert's grasp of American history that extended to baseball. Ken Burns' baseball series had fascinated him: "This program I watched in Chicago on that station with no commercials. It was wonderful. Joe Dimaggio. And another guy. Tall and white. Wilson?...Williams. Ted Williams. Ah, Williams, what a hitter, though Dimaggio set all the records. But Babe Ruth, everyone knows Babe Ruth. These are baseball's luminaries. But what is it with today's players? Are they greedy? They make a million dollars a year. What's wrong with them?"

I hoped the opinionated Williams could deliver a few thoughts, but when I arrived at his museum in Citrus Hills at 10 A.M. the parking lot was empty. I cruised into Ted's reserved spot and saw that the museum was no longer open Mondays. I pressed my face against the glass doors and knocked, praying that a custodian or a ball boy, anyone, was there to give me a quick tour. The sweat marks I left on the glass provided some satisfaction but not enough to counter another calamity in Florida. It was fortunate I only had a wiffleball bat because I wanted to strike out against the Sunshine State and do some serious Hall-of-Fame hitting.

18

A FAN'S PROPOSAL

All those won glory in their own generation and
were the pride of their times. Some there are
who have left behind them a home to be com-
memorated in story. Others are unremembered; they
have perished as though they had never existed, as
though they had never been born...
—Ecclesiasticus 44:7-9

Dear Major League Baseball,
You have more to worry about than the present and
future of your sport. Your past, especially in Florida, is
like a decaying ballpark in the bad part of town.
Next time you're in Florida, visit Cedar Hill Cemetery in Daytona Beach. Napoleon Lajoie is buried
there. His marker is darkened by mold. If clean, it
would be among the most attractive of Hall-of-Fame
graves. Instead, it looks like a lithograph, the engraved
glove, ball, bats, and words barely visible through the
blackened muck.

Joe Tinker in Orlando's Greenwood Cemetery is in worse shape. He rests below a magnificent oak (now that is something deserving of a poem). The family marker is being swallowed by ferns. His stone, a small one, perhaps 16 x 8 x 8, looks like the Titanic. Because of the oak and fern, the top is covered with a half-inch of compost. FATHER is solidly emblazoned on the side. However, only the top half of each letter is visible because the stone has sunk at an ugly angle in Greenwood's fertile earth.

Heinie Manush in Sarasota and Ed Walsh in Pompano Beach are endangered by grass that is too thick and too long. Weeds stretch across Heinie's wife's stone.

But at least they have markers. Bill Klem, showing that umpires truly get no respect, doesn't even have one. The area beside his wife is empty. Oh, there's a casket in the ground, but no headstone or footstone. Or for that matter, no tombstone, rolling stone, key stone, or gall stone. Nothing. What happened? Administrators at Miami's Graceland Memorial Park say it never existed. "For whatever reason the wife chose not to

purchase a marker. Maybe she didn't want people to
know where he is." What was she worried about? Fren-
zied fans hurling fruit? Irate managers kicking dirt on
it? Angry players tossing out his despised nickname
Catfish?

"It's a shame," said a secretary, "that someone who
made such a mark in life has no mark."

It is a shame. The bulk of Hall-of-Fame graves in
Florida need additional care, as do isolated graves elsewhere. Remedies exist.

1) Decide to improve the situation. Don't say that
upkeep is the responsibility of the family or cemetery.
Family members leave the area and cemeteries may be
understaffed or unable to do the work or maybe they're
just negligent. Figures like Heinie and Nap and Bill
Klem and Jimmy Foxx (whose grave in Miami's Flagler
Memorial Park swarmed with ants) are part of
baseball's family. Their memories should be respected.

2) Find representatives from each area to look after
the grave. This would not be difficult. People will volunteer. I promise. People who would never consider
helping at a homeless shelter or in a Big Brothers program would jump at the chance to tend to, say, Fred
Clarke's grave. You'll have hundreds of volunteers.
Heck, I'll take Harry Hooper's in Aptos, California. The
graves don't need plastic baseball bats like Grover
Cleveland Alexander had in St. Paul, Nebraska, but
flowers would be nice once in a while, maybe when they
were born or died or debuted in the majors. After that,
just keep the weeds away and the grass cut. And make
sure there's no muck. It's disgusting.

3) Make sure everyone has a marker. Roger Connor is also without one, as is Jimmy Collins.

4) Notify each cemetery and provide information on the Hall-of-Famer. The record, a few anecdotes, some photos. Heck, I'll do that, too.

5) Create a simple, uniform insignia to put on each grave. It needn't be flashy or obtrusive. There's no need for a Reggie Jackson- or Barry Bonds-type insignia. Ray Dandridge has a nice one on his crypt. It's only a couple of inches big and is as far from ostentatious as Candlestick is from Fenway. It's a badge of honor, an acknowledgement of membership in a select club. The military does it with its zillions of former servicemen. You can do the same for those who have served baseball.

Sincerely,

A Fan

19

FRIENDSHIP

A friend is one to whom one may pour out all the contents of one's heart—chaff and grain together—knowing that the gentlest of hands will take and sift it, keep what is worth keeping, and with a breath of kindness, blow the rest away.
—Arabian Proverb

Have you ever noticed how the pursuit of a foul ball is the perfect metaphor for the way individuals gain success in America? The struggle is often Social Darwinism at its unsocial best, but not always. Some gain their prize through diligence, toil, and ability, others by happenstance and luck, still others by inheritance—someone else does the work and hands down the prize in a gift of philanthropic bluster or selfless parental love. At first, it would seem everyone has the same chance for the ball. In reality, some are better situated or more talented or luckier or bigger or quicker. And sometimes the beer guy gets in the way.

I never saw him. The ball headed for the stands behind the first-base dugout. I kept my eyes on it as I glided Ozzie Smith-like (hey, it's my story) toward the aisle. En route to what would have been a difficult catch at best, I stumbled, crashed into the beer vendor, and tumbled down two steps. The vendor was down too and yelled something about the $3 brew he spilled. It's too expensive anyway, I thought, muttering an apology and trying to hide my hobble and embarrassment as I returned to my seat.

Both knees were bleeding, the left one badly, a series of scratches shone on each shin, my left hip was banged up, and I had pulled a butt muscle. My feet were still far from healed from the fire ant attack and my limbs were filling with bug bites from the moist South Carolina air. At this rate, I doubted I would survive the trip.

Even worse, I didn't come close to the ball.

My friend Peter was oddly ambivalent to my plight. He concentrated on the game, a Sally League contest between Columbia's Capital City Bombers and the Piedmont Phillies. My press pass got us in free. It is from 1983 when I worked on a Manteca, California, newspaper that folded in 1991, but is still acknowledged by media officers. Years ago I removed its expiration date and have since used it dozens of times for games and field access at Candlestick Park. Getting free admission, eating free food in the press box, and hanging out on the field during batting practice and in the locker room after games have been my small protest against the cost of tickets, although seeing Ken Oberkfell's mostly naked body on his way to the shower was Major League Baseball's cruel retribution.

Peter was to be my photographer for the Columbia game but he forgot his camera. We met in Georgia in the summer of 1993 at a four-week National Endowment for the Humanities Seminar titled "Virtue, Happiness and the Common Good in Plato's *Republic.*" We spent more time engrossed in the *Atlanta Constitution*'s and *New York Times*' sports pages than studying Socrates' polemic on the Cave. Our true debate was not the possibility of a philosopher-king or the chance of justice in society. We argued about Justice all right—Justice in the outfield and whether he was better than Bonds. Our two teams, Peter's Braves and my Giants, fought for the National League West title, and in that battle friendship was formed.

Much has been written of baseball's timelessness, but its calm is so often overlooked. The game permits, even encourages, conversation. Like the best relationships, baseball is made up of seemingly innocuous stretches interrupted by zaps of excitement and frenzy. Too much of the first—Joltin' Joe and Modelin' Marilyn, for example—and it dies of entropy. An overdose of the latter causes burnout. Madonna and a cast of dozens come to mind.

Baseball and life are often routine. And then you notice the little things. Infielders obscuring an open mouth to signal who'll cover second. A child's mural on a freeway overpass. A relief pitcher scurrying to warm up. The lighting in black-and-white movies. On-deck hitters timing pitches. Her eyes, a darker brown than you remembered. The grass, a more brilliant green than you thought possible. The smell of a barbecue.

You look forward to the big event—graduation,

driver's license, the wedding, the kid—just as you fear it—dropping out, the accident, divorce, the kid. Life matters most in the in-between times. The battle is won before the war. Friendships are nurtured in calm and forged in crisis. Peter's and my shared crisis was the train wreck of the 1994 season. We were at peace now, sharing our affair of the game.

Over the Fourth of July weekend we were like two kids opening the magic gift of baseball for the first time. We sought ways to get Peter's Rotisserie team out of the cellar. We visited the site of Ted Williams' future grave in Columbia's Elmwood Cemetery. We watched baseball highlights until our eyes drooped. We fed quarters into a batting cage long after our arms, hands, and fingers ached. During the Bombers' game we selected players we would most like to team with. They weren't necessarily the best players, just our favorites. Oh, we had to be on the team, too. The lineups:

Peter's Team	My Team
Brooks Robinson, 3B	Jackie Robinson, 1B
Honus Wagner, SS	Me, SS
Willie Mays, CF	Willie Mays, CF
Joe Jackson, LF	Ted Williams, LF
Roberto Clemente, RF	Roy Campanella, C
Rogers Hornsby, 2B	Brooks Robinson, 3B
Stan Musial, 1B	Minnie Minoso, RF
Yogi Berra, C	Nellie Fox, 2B
Peter, P	Satchel Paige, P

Willie and Brooks might have trouble playing for each team, but not as much as John McGraw would have managing. We each selected Mac to pilot our squads. Nellie is the ideal number two hitter, but no way will I bat eighth on my own team.

We also played wiffleball. It's difficult finding people my age to play wiffleball anymore. Reasons are never given, but I'm sure it has something to do with maturity and proper behavior for adults, and besides that, the arm's shot. Well, our arms were shot, too, so we made adjustments, lobbing our throws to the plate. But there was no teeing off on each grooved pitch; that would be too easy. Instead, the batter had to state where he would hit the ball, whether it was a single up the middle, a double to left-center, or a home run to right. If he failed, an out was recorded. The game was energetic and competitive. It matched the '62 Giants against the '95 Braves, who won 1-0 on Peter's called shot that landed on the lawn across the street. Of course, each plate appearance featured a called shot.

Finally, in the spirit of the Boston Tea Party, where British ships were vandalized for what some colonists considered a greater purpose, we perpetrated our own act of vandalism. Early one morning we spray painted a pitching rubber and homeplate into the middle of the street in front of Peter's house. It was no ballpark in the midst of corn, but in its own way it was just as powerful. Technically, I suppose, it was vandalism, although Peter argued it increased his property value. I had to agree. Anyway, it wasn't my property.

A neighbor, an old woman with the spirit of McGraw, rushed from her home across the street to inquire what we were up to.

"I saw y'all playing an' thought you were two boys,"

she said. "I was gonna run you off for being in the street and saw you were men. Whachall doin'?"

"Just playing some wiffleball, Mrs. Brush," Peter explained.

"I thought you were crazy."

"Well, my friend is from California."

"I don't want to see you layin' in the street. I ain't gonna come out and help y'all."

She was snappy and fiery and I didn't know if she was serious. Then, she winked at me. Appreciating her energy, I asked if she would like to take a few swings. She did not hesitate. She grabbed the yellow plastic bat and waved at the first pitch. She belted the next pitch through the box. I had to bust her inside on my next offering but she fought it off. A real-life Granny Hamner!

She made her way home, admonishing us about one thing or another. "Y'all better be careful." I doubt she ever took her own advice, and when I'm that age I hope I don't either. Even if it means tumbling down steps for a chance at a foul ball.

20

THE SCOUT MEETS THE MUTE

Insist on yourself. Never imitate.
—John Muir

Shoeless Joe had to emerge from cornfields in *The Field of Dreams*. It couldn't have been rye or tobacco or cotton or, God forbid, soybeans. Drive through the cornfields of the Northeast or Midwest or of southwestern Pennsylvania and you'll understand. You'll also understand why the Mayans worshipped corn, why corn was as important in their society as mirrors and television are in ours. The fields are a vast ocean of green. Prayers to the heavens.

The Mayans took their corn seriously. They took their games seriously, too. There was a connection. The Mayans played a ferocious contest—literally a life and death game—called Poktatok: part soccer, part basketball, part sacrificial offering. The goal was to knock a small, rubber ball through a stone hoop positioned vertically. Players used feet, knees, hips, and elbows to score; no throwing the ball through.

A member of the losing team, let's call him Tommy Lasorda, was placed on a stone altar. The victorious captain cut into the chest and pulled out the heart. Lasorda was removed and his heart set in a shallow groove on the altar. Blood (clearly not Dodger blue) streamed down the stone. It served as a sacrifice to the gods. Sorry, Tommy, sometimes you've got to take one for the team.

It was impossible to not think of the Mayans in Pennsylvania. The hills of the Monongahela Valley would fit perfectly in Guatemala. I was in Charleroi, a town of 5,700, that could have been transplanted from Central America. It was built amongst the hills, a quilt of homes—olive, blue, maroon, beige, white—with real life forest green trim. I stayed at a hostel downtown which gave decent access to the Pittsburgh graves: Traynor, Wagner, Gibson, and Galvin. As an extra bonus, a Colt League Tournament was scheduled that July 7-9 weekend.

Pittsburgh, PA July 10, 1995

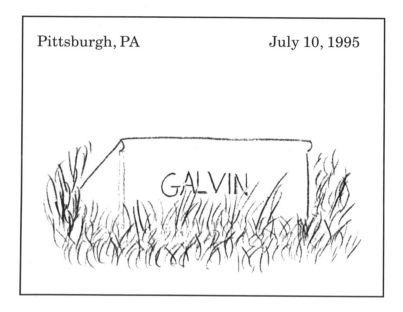

The first game I watched was tight in the middle innings. Down by a run, the home team wasn't hitting. The manager was increasingly irritable—Lou Pinella on PMS—and I wandered over to snoop on his advice to his 15- and 16-year-old players.

"Knock the shit out of the ball. I'm sick of this shit. Now hit the shit out of the ball. You can't win a damn ballgame with two dinky hits. It's right down the middle. Not on the inside corner, not on the outside corner. Now hit the damn ball."

They didn't. I returned to my seat for the final two innings. A woman repeatedly glanced at my notebook, which I shielded deftly. Her husband asked, "Are you a scout?"

"Yes." The game continued, the field did not open, nor did the heavens emit Kenesaw Mountain Landis,

his long, bony finger charging me with actions injuri-
ous to baseball. No, nothing like that, just the not so
subtle twirling of a dozen heads from a dozen necks.

"For who?"

"It's a scouting co-op for the major league teams on
the West coast. Dodgers, Angels, Giants, A's, Padres,
Mariners."

"What do you look for?"

"At this age, potential for growth and attitude are
the main things. You can't teach that."

The man nodded. His son was pitching. And losing,
despite his manager's hitting stratagem.

I savored my stint as scout. The people around me
listened closely. I discussed life on the road, its wariness and excitment, freedom and loneliness, none of
which I had to imagine. After three years in the North-
west, the Pennsylvania-Ohio Valley was my new assignment, I explained. I was still adjusting to it.

The game was nearly over. Last inning, two outs
and, after two heaters, an 0-and-2 count. The pitcher,
the couple's son, was up. The next pitch was a sloooow
curve.

Oh, you have to swing at those, son, too close to
take. Strike three. You're out. Game over. The boy
screamed. He slammed his bat to the ground and
frisbeed his helmet to the fence. Definitely a major
league tantrum.

What a shame. He had potential. I opened my notebook, shook my head mournfully, and jotted down a few
comments. Beside me I felt Mom's horrified glance.
Beside her, Dad whined, moaned, and sniped about the
umpiring.

Between games I biked downtown, riding four or five blocks against traffic on a one-way street, dodging a car on the way. I was in front of the hostel, fumbling with my lock when the first punch came. My right forearm was sore for days. The follow-up was a punch to my chest as I faced the attacker.

He was large, about 6'2," maybe 40-years-old, with an uncomfortable resemblance to Joe Stalin. More important, he was agitated and on his way to fury. He gestured wildly, pointing often toward the street I'd just been on. His mouth moved in angry silence except for occasional rasps.

He was a mute.

We stood on the corner of Main Street, my bike separating speaking and non-speaking worlds. He held a pad of paper in his right hand, but he had either forgotten it or was too angry to use it. Maybe he was the security guard and wanted me to lock my bike elsewhere. I prayed for intervention. My body tightened in fear, or nervousness, the kind you get when you're about to be made into a fool.

"Can you hear me?"

He nodded.

"Then, write it down."

The scrawl looked like that of one of my poorer eighth-grade students: "You need to follow traffic rules. If I would have hit you, the police would have gotten me."

Ah, the car I had dodged. "Well, that's true, I do need to obey traffic rules, but that doesn't give you the right to hit me."

He disagreed with succinct body language, shaking a fist inches from my face.

"If you're not going to be reasonable about this, then I'm not going to discuss this anymore."

He hoisted the bike, a 15-speed Myata, by seat and handlebars and slammed it down twice. Non-communication was perhaps the wrong approach.

I told him I'd call the police and he gestured that that would be just fine. The police were perhaps the wrong approach, too. Who would they side with? An unshaven Californian traveling the country looking for graves or the town mute? The man walked down the block, apparently in search of an officer. Leaving was undoubtedly the right approach. I mounted my bike.

"I hope you're not planning on riding that bike on the sidewalk."

A kid, a teenager, about 16, but small for his age, stood beside me. He wore a bright, orange shirt and a sick smile.

"You can't ride on the sidewalks here?" I asked. "They're strict about that?"

"Yes, they are. They got someone the other day. It's $200."

"They'll ticket you for riding on the sidewalk?" What kind of town was this?

"Or I'll ticket you."

"You? Who are you?"

"I'm town security." He showed me his badge, which I figured was fake, but I wasn't $200 positive. I muttered my thanks, walked the bike to the street, and rode in search of a police station to make a pre-emptive statement against my acquaintances. This was no way to treat a major league scout.

21

ALL-STARS

I wish I'd been born a second baseman.
—Tallulah Bankhead

Baseball players are no different than other performers. We're all actors, when you come right down to it, so I always thought I had to put a little acting into the game—you know, make it a little more interesting for the fans. So, whenever a ball was hit to center field, I'd try to time it right and get under the ball just in time to make the catch. It always made the play look a little more spectacular.
—Willie Mays

Why doesn't the American public direct its fury at movie stars? As I watched the All-Star Game, my favorite sporting event, I tried to comprehend that. Since 1969, I'd missed the game only once and I have a legitimate excuse: a summer of construction work in Poland in 1985.

Recently, though, I had struggled to catch it. In 1993, I entered bars throughout Guatemala City in search of a TV that had the game. I returned to my hotel, defeated, the odor of that afternoon's visit to the garbage dump trailing me like Pigpen's dust. As I walked to my room, I heard the faint cheers of a crowd. I traced them to a downstairs room and knocked on the door. A Peace Corps volunteer answered. Sorry to bother you but I'm a big baseball fan and I never miss the All-Star Game and I was wondering if I could maybe just watch a little of the game please and I'm really not a strange person or some kind of sicko it's just that this is something I look forward to every year and if your goal is to alleviate human suffering and better the world you'll do me this favor. He let me in, and I stayed for the final six innings. Thank God that John Kennedy, whose two baseball namesakes came as close to playing in the All-Star Game as they did of advising the president on the Bay of Pigs invasion, created the Peace Corps.

In 1994, I was at Princeton University, gathering information for a history lesson titled "Corsets and the Painful Cost of Beauty." There were no televisions in the dorm so I walked a few miles to a bar. Hoping to work while watching the game, I brought my research information with me, including two books: *The History of Underclothes* and *Fashion and Fetishism*. My knowledge of and comfort with drinking establishments is roughly opposite that of Babe Ruth's. I don't remember its name, but friends had told me it had atmosphere. Atmosphere is important in a bar, I suppose, although I'd much rather have free food.

I sat near the TV, ordered mineral water (straight up), set my notes and books in front of me, and watched the pre-game show. Two men huddled nearby talking baseball, or more accurately, mistalking. They mentioned Thomas when they meant Fielder, Bobby Bonds rather than Barry, Glavine instead of Maddux. This was worse than screeching blackboards or water tortures. Calm down, calm down, I told myself. Don't worry about it. Don't say anything. It was terrible. It was a pianist playing your favorite concerta, the one that brings you close to God, that helps you escape, that makes everything right with the world, but she keeps hitting the wrong—THE WRONG!—note.

"Remember when the Mets beat Baltimore in '68?"

Ignore it. These men are not the type who appreciate correction.

"Yeah, even though Robinson had that great Series."

Drink your mineral water. Watch the TV. Relax.

"Robinson was great but Eddie Murphy, he was my favorite."

Stop it, stop it. Please, stop it. Play the right note. Please, please play the right note.

"Eddie Murray."

They looked at me.

"Eddie Murray was the Orioles' player, Eddie Murphy is the actor, and Robinson had the great Series in 1970 against the Reds. The Mets beat Baltimore in 1969."

I spoke rapidly. If I were to get beat up, at least let the record be made straight.

They were more suspicious than angry. Their

conversation went on with more mistakes than the Dodgers' infield. Whenever they were in doubt, they looked at me. If they were correct (remember, even Hal Lanier homered once in a while), I nodded. If they were wrong, I gave the appropriate year or name. I didn't nod very much.

But this summer I was in Gettysburg, where Eddie Plank is buried in Evergreen Cemetery. Plank's grades from the Fall 1899 term were displayed in the Gettysburg State College library: 53 in Arithmetic, 70 in U.S. History, 65 in Physics, and 100 in Deportment. After taking a much needed swim in the Holiday Inn pool, I reserved the hotel's big screen TV in the lounge. The bartender laughed when I ordered a strawberry daiquiri, telling me it was a feminine drink. No matter. The introductions would begin soon.

"From the Great Lone Star State we welcome..."

Texans never tire of mentioning they used to be a separate nation or a republic and how no other state can fly its flag at the same level as the stars and stripes. The state possesses a massive insecurity complex. They brag incessantly about the Alamo, a battle they not only lost but were slaughtered in. It's a bit like Wall Street using Black Thursday and the Great Depression as its rallying cry for investors. The Lone Great Thing I noticed at the Alamo after seeing Rube Waddell's and Ross Youngs' graves in San Antonio was a sprawling oak tree of the Texas-sounding genus *Overcus Virginiana*.

Or to put the state's feelings another way, there

was this headline from the *Houston Chronicle*'s sports
section on January 28, 1962—"Baseball Hall of Fame:
2 Texans, 86 Other Guys."

I was anxious for the introductions to start. I love
the introductions and the tapestry of different uniforms. The All-Star Game is the athletic version of the
Oscars. The cameras zoom in on the stars, past and
present. Are not Joe Dimaggio and Jimmy Stewart cut
from the same cloth? Years removed from their greatest successes, they are legends, more warmly received
and more cherished than the youngsters. And when
you're 80, everyone is a youngster.

The cameras shift to the mainstays. Puckett in his
10th game, Boggs in his 11th, the acrobatic Ozzie
Smith in his 14th. Can't you see James Earl Jones, Mel
Gibson, and Morgan Freeman in their spikes?

Players enter, stages left and right. Their idiosyn-
crasies and traits and mannerisms so evident.
Dykstra's chew & spit tobacco dance. Gwynn's belly.
Nomo's motion. Gant's arms. Piazza's stats. Thomas'
size. Johnson's tumbling hair. Bonds' earring and that
weird way he chokes up. The mild-mannered Maddux.

The show begins and the cameras focus on the first-
timers, those we've heard about but seen little of.
Conine, Biggio, Alou. Relaxed, happy, enjoying the
show. It must be great to get your first nomination
when you're young. They're the future, you know. They
really didn't pay their dues, not like David Wells or
Ontiveros. Those guys have been around forever, probably figured they'd never make the team, they must
really appreciate it.

Suddenly Don Zimmer and his gnarled fist of a face are on the screen. I didn't know he was still alive. What a great character actor he was. The best. He was marvelous in *Popeye*.

The emcees reminisce and inform. Dennis Martinez and Heathcliff Slocumb. Oh, those heartbreak stories, those examples of courage and fortitude. Alcohol almost impeached *El Presidente,* but he kicked it, you know. And what about that Slocumb? Losing his wife and father in the same year. How do you go on from that? How do you?

Bill Plummer. Out of the blue the emcee mentions Bill Plummer. Bill Plummer? That name is familiar. He was in, uh, wasn't he in *Reds*, no, no, it was, God, it's on the tip of my tongue. I got it. *The Sound of Music*. He was Captain Von Trapp...Shoot, that was Christopher Plummer. Wait, he was one of the crooks in *All the President's Men*, ah, geez, I don't know, but he was someone. I know that name. It's gonna drive me crazy.

And talk about crazy. Look, they're bringing in that Carlos Perez character from Montreal. Look at that strut, an' did you ever see a dance like that on stage? What an act. What'll the guy do next? Ah, they're taking him out. Don't take him out. Leave him in, this is entertainment, dammit. No one gives Cher the hook when she has the spotlight. The hair, the clothes, the attitude. That's entertainment. That's what we want to see when we watch The Show.

Hack Wilson, who died penniless at the end of his troubled life, has one of the most ostentatious graves, while the great and humble Walter Johnson (opposite page) is buried simply. Wilson is in Martinsburg, West Virginia, and Johnson is in Rockville, Maryland.

22

A BETTER DAY

Even if your night's shelter is uncertain
and your goal still far away
know there doesn't exist
a road without an end—
don't be sad.
—Hafiz

On March 7, 1995, Leon Day, who never played a Major League game in his life, was selected to the Baseball Hall of Fame.

His friend and fellow Negro Leaguer Max Manning recalled the day. "'Buddy, you made it.' And Leon got tears in his eyes."

Six days later, Leon died. He was 78. When I arrived at Arbutus Memorial Park in Baltimore four months later, his grave had no marker. An installation ceremony was scheduled in a week, on July 23.

That would give me enough time to visit graves in Delaware, Philadelphia, and New Jersey before

attending the ceremony. The trip was a painful one for I had fallen hard and suddenly for a woman in Washington, D.C. She was cute and fun and intelligent, and I felt we had much in common. Which we did, including, unfortunately, an affinity for women. The news of her lesbianism struck me as unfair, but it shouldn't have surprised me. During one of our first conversations, we discussed which character from Gilligan's Island we would most like to spend an uncharted week with. We both chose Mary Ann.

The beauty of the northeastern landscape, especially the eternal cornfields that I never tired of, now
only made me lonely. No matter how full the tank, no
matter how much I ate or read, I was empty and
thought only of her when I saw something lovely, and
because I was in some of the most beautiful country of
the trip, that meant I thought of her constantly.

The heat exacerbated my misery. Waiting in air-
conditioned offices while secretaries searched for
burial information was sweeter than the perfect kiss.
Walking among the tombstones became arduous. Even
drawing lost its normal joy. I am artistically retarded
at best but, for whatever reasons, was able to do re-
spectable renderings of the graves. Using colored pen-
cils, I spent 15 minutes to an hour at each site,
carefully sketching the stone into a book a student
gave me as a farewell gift. As a result, I created a more
personalized record of my journey and gave myself a
chance to slow down and reflect.

There was no reflecting the heat, however. Sweat
dripped onto the drawings and my hand stuck to the
pages as if they were vinyl. Life had become a series of
cemeteries, maps, mediocre food, and gas stations in a
humid broth. At times I forgot where I was. Mentally
backtracking, I searched for a clue that would tell me
what state I was in. I was dazed and doubted I would
complete the trip, especially after suffering heat stroke
from a three-hour stint searching for and sketching
John McGraw's, Wilbert Robinson's, and Joe Kelley's
graves in Baltimore's New Cathedral Cemetery.

It was already mid-July and I'd seen fewer than 50
graves. Another 100 remained. One-fifth of those were

John McGraw's crypt in Baltimore's New Cathedral Cemetery. Its inscription: BLESSED ARE THE DEAD WHO DIE IN THE LORD.

in Boston and New York City, which loomed like Ted Williams and Babe Ruth to a haggard, weak-armed pitcher who had suddenly lost his stuff. I was that pitcher. And with the bases loaded and the heart of the order approaching, I cringed when the scoreboard showed it was only the top of the fourth in the biggest game of my life. There was no calling the bullpen.

I surged on, summoning strength from the misfortunes of others, gaining hope from those who have toiled beyond human limits. The Middle Passage. The Bataan Death March. The Donner party. The Titanic. George Keegan, an Englishman who spent over seven years walking from Tierra del Fuego to Alaska, by way of the East Coast, a distance of 28,000 miles. Or any person who has driven cross country with children. Hellish, back-breaking journeys, all worse than mine. If others survived, I could too.

The service was scheduled to start in 25 minutes. I pulled off the road near the cemetery to change. Throughout the trip my wardrobe consisted of shorts and T-shirts, so I had borrowed clothes from my friend David. It was too warm to wear his outfit during the

45-minute drive from his home in D.C., but I had neglected to try them on beforehand. The shirt fit fine, and then I tried the slacks. They rode three inches above my ankles, and when I sat, they rose to mid-shin, providing a view of my white socks and increasingly tanned legs. I had to wear them.

This was not David's first gaffe. He and his wife Lori teach at the prestigious National Cathedral School in Washington D.C. Their students have included Corinne Quayle, the three Gore girls, and Victoria Will, daughter of George, the political analyst and crazy Cubs fan. Will's politics are crazy, too, but he is well connected, albeit as off-center as a right fielder guarding the line, so I asked David to mention my trip, if he had the opportunity. Will was scheduled to speak to David's eighth-grade government class. He arrived a few minutes early.

"I didn't know what to say to him," David recalled. "There was this silence and it was very uncomfortable. And then I remembered you. I told him that my friend is writing a book about baseball. He got very excited."

"Oh, do you like baseball?" Will asked.

"No, frankly, I find it quite boring."

The moment ruined, Will was unenthusiastic and unresponsive when David explained my trip.

A half-dozen former Negro Leaguers attended Day's ceremony. I wanted to approach them, but I was too self-conscious about my pants. Lowering them to my hips was effective but only momentarily. Feeling like the only person in costume at a Halloween Party,

I sat at the far end of a row of folding chairs, stared at my exposed shins, and realized that I had no clue who Leon Day was. Did he pitch or play the field? If he pitched, did he throw heat or junk? What kind of record did he have? Was he wild? What about his pickoff move? Did he have a high leg kick or whip it from the side? And if he didn't pitch, where'd he play? And how'd he hit? With power? Was he fast? Flashy? Could he field? What did he accomplish?

The answer to at least the last question arrived when Leon's son sat in front of me. The back of his shirt was as helpful as a longer pair of pants. It read:

Born October 30, 1916
Died March 13, 1995
22 Year Career—Constantly Over .300
Beat Satchel Paige 3 out of 4 Games
Played a Record 7 East/West Championship Games
Holds the Record for 14 Strikeouts in
    East/West Games
Holds the Record for 18 Strikeouts in
    Negro Leagues
Holds the Record for 19 Strikeouts in Puerto Rico

The list continued, but the son sat back in his chair as the service began.

Two men spoke. Todd Bolton and Bob Hieronimus, both white, led the drive for Day's induction. Their efforts were admirable. They devote their lives to mainstream Negro League history, to make Pee Wee Butts as well known as Pee Wee Reese. But I was uncomfortable with their work. I am suspect of any popular movement. Hieronimus hopes the admittance of Turkey Stearns, Mule Suttles, and 20 to 30 others will not be as difficult as Day's. As Hieronimus spoke, I feared that some of these players are undeserving of Hall admittance. Perhaps they'll dilute the Hall of Fame even more than it currently is.

In his closing remarks, Bolden emphasized the need to right the wrongs, or to write the rights of the past. Day's "record was obscured by the prejudices of history...never again will his name be lost to history....(he now) has his proper place in history."

Baseball whiz Bill James has argued that honoring overlooked players is pointless. Who cares about Tony Mullane or George Davis, he says. James is wrong. There, I said it, I disagreed with baseball's god of analysis without getting a Louisville Slugger to the shins. James has made a living with the truth, with putting numbers in proper perspective. Players, even dead ones, even ones of long ago, need to be viewed at least as well as statistics. The Hall of Fame is to honor the greatest players, even those who have been overlooked for decades.

Leon is no longer among that group because it is a new day, a more equitable one. Unlike many of his fellow players and managers and opponents, he was able to enjoy it. For six days.

I visited the graves of Home Run Baker in Easton, Maryland, and Goose Goslin in Salem, New Jersey, on consecutive days in mid-July during the East Coast's fierce heat wave.

23

MATTY AND
THE GENERAL

*It healed the wounds of war, and was balm to
stinging memories of sword thrust and saber
stroke...And then, when true patriots of all sections
were striving to forget that there had been a time of
black and dismal war, it was a beacon, lighting their
paths to a future of perpetual peace.*
—Al Spalding on the merits of ballplaying

I felt like a model for a car magazine. Lori had me
posing with Nellie as though we were lovers. "Another
shot, just one more." Impatience gnawed at my frozen
smile. It was already 10 A.M., an hour later than my
hoped-for starting time, and it was hot. My time with
David and Lori had been glorious, like a return to college: late-night talks, lots of food, softball, movies, and
me still without a girlfriend.

But that could change. Peter in South Carolina and

David are both nerdy history types who didn't find
their mates until their 30s. There was hope, although
hoping that a 30-year-old woman would change her
gender preference is not what you'll want to risk next
month's rent on, or even today's laundry money.

I craved to be traveling again, anxious for the freedom of the road. Though I'd been treated like a king at
the homes of friends, true power belongs to the nomad.
Free again, except for my infatuated heart, I drove
north. The countryside was once more tortuous in its
beauty, especially the Susquahanna, the prettiest river
I've ever seen. A series of outcroppings gave its shallow
depths personality and perspective. After following its
calm for miles, I was suddenly struck by the obvious: as
much as I loved it, as much as I desired it, I could never
have it.

I don't know where my love of rivers came from.
There were none near me growing up in Santa Clara,
California. But I never tired of seeing them or crossing
them or soaking in them. They are strangely
exhilirating to cross and I crossed nearly every major
one—the Rappahannock and the Monongahela, the
Allegheny and Ohio and Tennessee, the Hudson and
Colorado and Columbia, the Missouri and the Mississippi (a dozen times, including twice on foot). They
exude more life than forests and more power than
mountains. They flow with excitement.

Christy Mathewson was certainly familiar with the
Susquahanna. He graduated from Bucknell College in
Lewisburg, Pennsylvania, which is built on the river's

banks. He is buried in the city cemetery, an easy walk to the campus where Matty was a three-sport star. He was loyal to his alma mater and loyal to his country, enlisting to serve in World War I. The decision would eventually kill him, as was the case with decisions made by other good, decent, likable young men. The cemetery spoke of that. American flags were everywhere, fluttering appreciation to those who served and died.

The war was over when Christy went to Europe as part of the Army of the Occupation. He was already 38 when he left as Reds manager to lead and work with the U.S. Chemical Service. Christy was accidentally exposed to poisonous gas, when he should have been putting together a less hazardous staff. (Cincy pitchers had the league's second highest earned run average in 1918.) Tubercolosis set in and his health never returned. The man who prided himself on reaching back for his best stuff in tight situations could not reach back far enough in this one. He died seven years later at the age of 45.

His grave omits any mention of his brilliant pitching record. Only his war record appears, including the odd emblem of the USCS—what looks like two golf clubs crossed over an oval.

Christopher Mathewson, Jr., is also in the family plot. He followed his dad's footsteps. Young Christopher was a colonel in the U.S. Air Force and died in the Korean War. He was 44. Boys and their wars. Wife and mother Jane Stoughton Mathewson (1880-1967) surely buried both. Even with the bronze Daughters of American Revolution emblem and American flag at her grave, could she have viewed the loss of husband and son a worthwhile sacrifice?

It had been an emotional day—the dwelling on
impossible love, the confrontation with early, unnecessary death. I went to the local library for rest. Libraries
were my comforting angels: air-conditioned mostly,
friendly, helpful people, clean bathrooms, and heaven-
sent furniture. I tracked down a copy of Mathewson's
Pitching in a Pinch and slumped into a chair. Some of
the more interesting passages:

Schoolboys of the last ten years have been acquainted with the exact figures which have made up Matty's pitching record before they had ever heard of George Washington because George didn't play in the same league.

Evers and McGraw got into a conversation one day in the deaf and dumb language at long range and "Johnny" Evers threw a finger out of joint replying to McGraw in a brilliant flash of repartee.

The future of the game depends on the umpire, for his honesty must not be questioned. If there is a breath of suspicion against a man, he is immediately let go, because constant repetition of such a charge would result in baseball going the way of horse racing and some other sports.

The only good umpire is a dead umpire. (Attributed to McGraw)

Another great piece of luck is for a ball-player to rub a colored kid's head. I've walked along the street with ball-players and seen them stop a young negro and take off his hat and run their hands through his kinky hair. Then I've

*seen the same ball-player go out and get
two or three hits that afternoon and play
the game of his life.*

I needed luck the following day, July 26, to find
Bucky Harris and Hugh Jennings, and got it from an
unlikely source, which was not my Hall-of-Fame list.
Compiled by a pair of associate researchers at the Hall
who should have been put on waivers, the list was increasingly error prone. Some were minor inconve-
niences such as the misnaming of cemeteries. Others
were more troublesome—listing the wrong city, for
example. Or in the case of Leon Day, having him buried
in Sulphur Spring, Maryland, a city that does not exist;
Leon is buried in Baltimore's Arbutus Memorial Park
on Sulphur Spring Road. Herb Pennock, meanwhile,
was listed in New York City, a mere 80 miles from his
actual resting place in Kennett Square, Pennsylvania.
The most egregious error, the Bill Buckner of errors,
would not surface until the trip's final day on my
penultimate stop.

When officials in Pittston, Pennsylvania, had no
knowledge of Harris' whereabouts, I assumed the list
was wrong again. They directed me to State Representative Tommy Tigue in neighboring Hughestown.
Tigue was happy to help, but I wondered how happy he
was while sweating in his coat and tie. We were in a de-
ceivingly large graveyard connected to St. Peter's
Lutheran Church less than a block from Tigue's Rock
Street office. Tigue was in his eighth term serving the
118th Legislative District. He served with the Marines
in Vietnam and now worked on committees overseeing

Military Affairs and Emergency Preparedness, Finance, Labor Relations, and Democratic Policy. Most impressively, his daughter is married to a major league pitcher, the Padres' Andy Ashby.

I found the marker, a small, unspectacular one. Tigue and I returned to his office. He gave me a can of lemonade and asked about my next stop.

"St. Catherine's Cemetery in Scranton. Hughie Jennings is there."

Tigue looked troubled. He was unfamiliar with such a cemetery in nearby Scranton. He made a few calls, finally locating St. Catherine's in Moscow (20 minutes beyond Scranton), and confirmed that Jennings was there. This was government intervention at its best—a drink, a few calls, stomping around in the trenches—and I wasn't even one of his constituents.

He was eager to learn about my trip. Where have you been? What is the South like? What's the prettiest part of the country? His excitement was genuine.

"I would love to do what you're doing," he said. "I've often thought I would like to be a truck driver for two years, just driving and seeing the country."

Tigue was representative of hundreds of people I met. Their enthusiasm for my journey was a constant help, like a father's watchful hands hovering near his wobbly son who discards his training wheels for the first time.

As twilight passed that night, I floated on the Delaware River and watched trees turn to silhouettes. I was about 90 miles upriver of the spot where a 44-year-old general surreptitiously crossed on Christmas night 219 years before. The surprise attack was a rare success for the leader, George Washington, who led his rebel forces in their fight for independence from Britain.

Washington, of course, survived the Battle of Trenton to serve two terms as president and to have the misfortune of the Senators carrying his name a century after his death. He could have died much earlier. After leading 150 men into a skirmish in 1754, Washington wrote that he "heard the bullets whistle, and, believe me, there is something charming about the sound."

Amidst the peace of the Delaware, hearing only my gentle efforts to stay afloat, I understood young George's fascination with music-making death. War is an opportunity to fully live, or die trying. If it weren't for the killing, it'd be great. War stretches physical and emotional and spiritual limits, while destroying the routine of modern life where there is little action, little happiness, little aliveness.

For the first time as an adult, for the first time since I wrestled in high school, my limits were being tested. The miles and weather were taking a toll. There was joy in this, though, even when bullets sped toward me. In my aloneness I was buoyed by my escape from comfort and ease where limits whither like a retired pitcher's throwing arm. Caressed by the river's lapping calm, I could accept my respite for what it was: another part of being fully alive as I watched another day fade away.

24

LOU AND THE BABE

It is not the honor that you take with you,
but the heritage you leave behind.
—Branch Rickey

Poor Lou Gehrig. How is it that a man who in life
was overlooked, overshadowed, over everything but
overrated could have the same problems in death? He
played alongside the Babe, which meant he had as
much chance of getting his due as a mime opening for
the Beatles. When Ruth left, Gehrig had a year to himself, a very ordinary year as it turned out (30, 119,
.329). Could the limelight have been distracting, even
though it was rationed with future Hall-of-Famers
Gomez, Dickey, Ruffing, Combs, and Lazerri? A year
later, 1936, a rookie named Dimaggio joined the team,
catching everything in sight, including the headlines
and hearts. It is well known that Lou couldn't even
dominate the papers on his biggest moment in baseball. He smacked four homers against Philadelphia on

the day John McGraw retired as manager and icon of the New York Giants. Of course, Lou is probably better known for being overshadowed (and for his disease) than had he received his proper due.

Gehrig is one of several luminaries in Valhalla's Kensico Cemetery, less than an hour from New York City. Danny Kaye and Ayn Rand are buried there. So are Tommy Dorsey and Sergei Rachmaninoff. Husband and wife Florenz Ziegfield and Billie Burke (Glinda the Good) are too. Gehrig isn't even the lone baseball figure at Kensico (no relation to Jose). Another Hall-of-Famer, former Red Sox manager and Yankee general manager Ed Barrow roots not too far from the Iron Horse.

Valhalla, NY   July 27, 1995

BARROW

And Col. Jacob Ruppert, Yankees owner during their dynastic days in the '20s and '30s, is there as well. In fact, the cemetery guide explains how Gehrig missed spring training in 1935 because of Ruppert: "Gehrig was holding out for an annual salary of

$40,000, but Ruppert thought the first baseman was worth only $39,000. Gehrig eventually accepted Ruppert's offer."

The Colonel's penury is understandable. Gehrig was coming off a season in which he failed to finish among the league leaders in triples or even stolen bases. He did, however, manage to capture the triple crown (49, 145, .363) and lead the American League in total bases, slugging percentage, and on-base percentage. He was runner-up in hits, doubles, and walks and third in runs scored.

Lou's headstone, which he shares with wife Eleanor, was, like the man, solid but unspectacular. Small American flags fluttered on each side of the grave and someone had left a gift of a new pro model Yankee cap. Good for Lou. Someone had honored him with what, until then, was the nicest offering I'd seen. There'd been a couple of plastic bats and a wiffleball near Grover Cleveland Alexander's grave. And a ball that looked as though it had run through a series of

tests with kitchen appliances lay on Dizzy Dean's stone. The cap, though, the cap was something special.

I was anxious to see Ruth's grave, which was less than five minutes away in Gate of Heaven Cemetery in Hawthorne. The Babe is clearly the cemetery's star, standing above fellow residents Sal Mineo, James Cagney, Westbrook Pegler, and Billy Martin. A stuffed bunny (!) looked haggard and infinitely out of place beneath Martin's inscription:

*I may not have been the greatest Yankee
to put on the uniform but I was the proudest.*

The greatest Yankee, no, the greatest player, was
30 feet away. The monument was immense, as large
and as unique as the man. Two figures were carved in
relief, including Jesus, who has more saves than Lee
Smith, Rollie Fingers, and Hoyt Wilhelm put together.
Jesus' strength showed through his robes as he looked
upon a defiant youngster, angry, dressed in a baseball
uniform. The figures stare at each other, one with compassion and understanding, the other daring anyone to
love him. It takes only a little knowledge of Ruth's
childhood—the incorrigible George, the days spent in
his father's bar and on Baltimore's wild docks, the
stints in reform school under the care of Franciscan
brothers—to know who the figures represent: Babe as
a boy and the imposing Father Mathias, whom Ruth
considered "the greatest man I ever knew."
    Ruth's greatness has transcended eras. His grave
has become an altar. It receives 5-10 visitors daily, pil-
grims leaving offerings of love and appreciation. With
four baseballs and a cracked Louisville Slugger it had
the look of a sporting goods store. But there was more:
51 cents, a Baby Ruth candy bar, four flags, and, finally, the messages:

*I wish you were alive today so that I could
meet you. I would shake your hand and get your
autograph. That would make any baseball fan happy.
Happy 100th!
Love Always,
Alison Berenbeck*

and

Babe, you were the greatest. We miss you.
Tro

and

You're still an inspiration to boys (& men)
across America.

and simply

Thank you, Babe

Baseball could use Babe now. His joy and boundless energy for autographs would be just what the commissioner ordered (if a real commissioner existed). But it is doubtful Ruth could survive in our climate.

If the Babe were baseball's savior, and after the Black Sox scandal he was, it is best that he not resurrect today as we near the millineum. His behavior would not play as mild antics. The women, the alcohol, the delights of the flesh, would lead to his excoriation. The press would vilify him, true, but he'd still have the headlines, always the headlines, and that's what Ruth needed to perform. The adulation was fuel to continue, fuel that continues at his altar in the form of gifts and worshipers.

Gehrig should not feel bad about being overshadowed by his teammate and this baseball god. He is not alone. A large crucified Christ is not far from Ruth's grave. No messages had been left, nor any gifts. Not even an Angels cap.

Wappingers Falls, NY   July 27, 1995

*Dan Brouthers is buried in a simple grave behind St. Mary's
Catholic Church in Wappingers Falls, New York.*

Brentwood, MD   July 21, 1995

*Clark Griffith's large vault in Brentwood, Maryland, on the
outskirts of Washington, D.C. A cemetery worker wanted to
take me inside but his key did not work.*

25

SOME TIME IN COOPERSTOWN

Heck, let's face it, I was just a big ol' country boy
havin' the time of his life. It was a lark to me, just a joy
ride…Why, I never even realized it was supposed to be
big doin's. It was just a game, that's all it was. They
didn't have to pay me. I'd have paid them to let me play.
Listen, the truth is it was more than fun. It was heaven.
—Goose Goslin

Cooperstown. The Hall of Fame. During the days preceding Induction Weekend, I heard and read countless times that this was what Baseball was all about. This was Baseball's roots, its Eden, its birthplace (never mind that this small, rural village has as much right claiming progeny of Baseball as do George Steinbrenner and Marge Schott, whose offspring would best be kept far from human contact). But while it is not Jerusalem, it is at least Mecca and it would help us forget about what's wrong with Baseball. The five work stoppages in 13 years. Greed as a creed. The whining millionaires. The lost World Series of '94. Redemption is possible, sayeth the acting commissioner. I hoped so because I still had not forgiven Baseball, or rather, I hadn't forgiven its participants.

I prayed for its destruction. I waited for it to collapse from within, for society to first ignore and then forget the stadiums, the replay screens, the hot dogs, cokes and popcorn, the Louisville Sluggers and split fingers, the pine tar and resin bags, the doubles in the gap and diving stops down the line, the intentional walks, the umpires and managers and players and owners, the booing and cheering and rooting, all of it, even the most beautiful of sights, the first glimpse of grass, so colorful that a crayon should be named for it. I wanted it forgotten in a rubble until one day, maybe a thousand, maybe two thousand years from now, a couple of kids serendipitously discover the peace of tossing a rock back and forth or learn the joy of smacking it with a stick on a sunny day with a slight breeze.

After an early morning drizzle, the weather in Cooperstown on Induction Eve was perfect, perfect for Baseball. And at the same time, it was horrible. For when the sun emerged, so did the autograph hounds and vendors. Sidewalk hawkers advertised their wares like they were part of a multicultural bordello. At Cooperstown, all was for sale: photos, bats, balls, lithographs, everything. Even the women got into the act. Their newfound fame from *A League of Their Own*

went for $20 per autographed ball. The sidewalk
screamers shouted where to purchase the delights. You
don't like our blond pitcher at 2, then try our red-
headed infielder at 3 or our Dominican Dandy at 4.
Something for everyone.

Feller, Killebrew, Spahn, Ford, Wilhelm, and Kell
were among the Hall-of-Famers selling. There was
also, according to a xeroxed schedule put out by someone named Jack Berke, a "rare appearance by Phillie
Legend and Future Hall of Famer Dick Allen." It's nice
that Mr. Berke clued us in to future Inductees. Orlando
Cepeda and Buck O'Neil are among them, I learned,
but Larry Christenson—Larry Christenson!?—and
Andy Seminick (whose name was misspelled on one
placard) are not. Perhaps they should charge more
than $8 an autograph if they want serious Hall consid-
eration.

The players aren't totally to blame for the atmosphere, perhaps not even mostly. The sports collectors
are the real culprits. Their stockpiling and marketing
of signed papers, balls, bats, and jerseys is pernicious.
In June I attended a Chattanooga Lookouts game and
watched a trio of sleazy, sallow-faced men slide card
after card to players for a quickie autograph. No eye
contact. No acknowledgment. No appreciation. No
thank you. Players should be upset that these creatures profit from their names. No doubt they would
have fought over Jesus' robes, prayed and fasted for his
resurrection, and then asked him to sign them.

I waited for the Babe to rise and wipe out the ped-
dlers as Jesus did in the temple. He didn't show, although a Babe Ruth impersonator did. "He was here

yesterday at the Wax Museum," said a 14-year-old boy, a Cooperstown native. "It was tacky."

Yes, this is what it was all about, and after I noticed a sign exhorting me to win a Willie Stargell Commemorative Mirror, I had seen enough. I like Stargell a lot, but would you want to wake up to him every morning while you flossed? Buc no.

I biked away from downtown to avoid the crowds. Security guards screened prospective visitors to the magnificent hotel set on the shore of Lake Otsego. They were part of an all-star contingent of guards from Syracuse, Rochester, and other New York cities. The Otsego is the place of choice for Hall-of-Famers and ex-players during Induction weekend, at least in large part because of its golf course. (Wouldn't it be odd if ex-golfers took up Baseball? Or in other words, imagine Arnie racing from first to third on Jack's single to right off Lee's heater.) I tried getting past the guards but was unsuccessful. It wasn't always this way.

"I was here for Brooks' induction," a Philadelphia man told me over breakfast at the Doubleday Cafe. "We ate lunch at the Otsego Hotel. We had a dozen baseballs. Willie Mays was at the table next to us and we said, 'Say, can you sign these?' 'Sure, fellas, anytime.' You could walk right up to them. This is crazy. I saw a ball yesterday with six Hall-of-Famer signatures on it for $500. I have a ball with 50 Hall-of-Famers."

About 20 Famers were on the golf course and at least 20 times that many people lined the three-foot high stone wall for a glimpse and, more important to them, a signature. They waited—with balls in plastic cubes, with cards in plastic casings, with bats in plastic

cylinders. I got the impression that if Harmon
Killebrew ever used their toilet, it'd be permanently
plastic wrapped.

I waited a while, listening to shameless pleadings
for autographs mixed with the occasional exploitation
of children. "Sign one for the kids, Scooter?" asked one
benevolent adult. Scooter did sign. So did Joe Morgan,
who chatted amiably, albeit distantly. Enos Slaughter
seemed to consider the fans annoying and did not sign.
Neither did several others who I couldn't get excited
about because I didn't recognize them. Is that old guy
with his left arm shooting off at the weird angle Spahn
or Newhouser? I could have been watching an AARP
outing on the links. I quickly bored of bird watching
(where was Brooks?), though I wouldn't have if
Cooperstown had mandated names on the backs of
polo shirts.

I questioned my decision to attend the festivities.
In 1995, this is what Baseball was all about: Fans pur-
suing contact from players desiring privacy and a reliable 3 iron. I crossed the street dejectedly. Was there
anything left of Baseball's soul? Was it foolish to spend
my time watching this game? I felt I was in love with a
woman who'd taken poor care of herself. I looked at the
flabby thighs, the hollow eyes, the obsession with
money and image and fame. How did I ever love her?
Did she still exist, buried but still there amidst the
cellulite, jewelry, and expensive perfume?

The Farmers' Museum was opposite the golf course.
It was an unlikely place for answers concerning Baseball. Heck, I doubted they even had the reaper that
mangled Mordecai Brown's hand, which resulted in

one of Baseball's greatest monikers. Without the machine, Three-Finger Brown would have been just another Farmer Brown.

A town ballgame was scheduled that afternoon, so I killed time in the museum. Are farmers from the heartland as apoplectic over shears, barbed wire, cheese presses, cheese sieves, cheese boxes, and sausage stuffers as Baseball fans are when they see Stuffy McInnis' bat in the town's other museum?

The other museum is magnificent but the $9.50 entrance fee deterred me. I'd been there before, and it was now too crowded with the busloads of Phillie fans arriving frighteningly often to revere Richie Ashburn and resume their love-hate relationship with Mike Schmidt. Besides, the town ballgame was about to start. Town ball is to Baseball what the Wright Brothers' (Wilbur and Orville, not George and Harry) first plane is to a 747. It looked a little wacky, but the ancestry was indisputable.

Town ball dates back to the early 1800s; its 21 rules were enacted as part of the Massachusetts Game in 1858. It is played on a square rather than a diamond. Four bases—each is actually a four-foot high stick—are set 60 feet apart. The striker (batter) stands equidistant between First and Fourth (Home) base. He faces the thrower 35 feet away and requests the location of his pitches, which are to be grooved. Can you imagine Bob Gibson or Drysdale operating under such a system?

There is no foul territory and only one out per frame. Outs are made either by catching balls on the fly (no diving, though, this is a gentlemen's game) or, more sadistically, by drilling a runner with the ball as he heads to a base. This is known as plugging or soaking. The ball need not be thrown softly—the game isn't that gentlemanly. Maybe Gibson and Drysdale would prefer this version after all, although the soft leather-coated, hand-sewn ball would not be to their liking.

I joined the players for warmups, playing catch with two eighth graders. Each throw alleviated some of my frustration over the silliness of commemorative mirrors that prevailed a few moments away. The ball was love in my hands and a gift to those who touched it. I was happy.

A dark green bench sat empty on a grassy knoll and made the perfect seat. The first breeze in days arrived. Sugar maples surrounded the oval shaped field. A few structures were visible, part of the museum's re-creation of a 19th century village. They included an apothecary, schoolhouse, and doctor's office and were built of flatstone, whose gray simplicity is native to New York and whose beauty rivals that of any stone.

Hand-hewn bats add to the atmosphere of town ball at Cooperstown.

The game began and the range in ability was immediately evident and the rule differences amusing. Baserunning was particularly odd as the game took on a look of The Keystone Cops Go To Wrigley. Tallies were made by circling the bases in sequential order, but on occasion strategy dictated that a runner go from third to second or even first. Running out of the baselines, in some cases running far out of the lines, was permissable. It was not unusual to have, say, the third striker in an inning score before the first striker. Where was Babe Herman or Marv Throneberry when you needed them?

Despite the oddities, it was Baseball: pitching, catching, hitting, running, scoring. It was the game's foundation as much as flesh, blood, bone, and muscle are the human foundation. But without heart or soul the body, as well as the game, is limp. Lifeless.

This game, these players, had life. Their joy was infectuous and it infected me. Major Leaguers have lost much of that joy. Just ask Barry Bonds who discussed retiring at age 31. Too often they look as though they're on the wrong side of the Spanish Inquisition.

An estimated 25,000 fans packed into Cooperstown that weekend, but only a few dozen watched the town ball game. From my elevated seat, I had a clear view of the golf course and occasionally looked toward the clamoring hordes seeking autographs from annoyed stars.

I felt sorry for both groups—the players and the fans. They were missing the point. Two hours breezed by too rapidly. I sat on the bench long after the game ended, savoring a piece of art and a revelation. I finally understood what Baseball was about, and it was about time.

26

LEGACY

Sarah Pryor was nine years old when she went for a walk on a beautiful October day in 1985 in Wayland, Mass. She never returned and…was never found. Sarah's mother Barbara fondly recalls winter mornings when Sarah was in elementary school. Each morning after a snow fall, Sarah would put on her snow gear and head out with her dog, Katie, to sneak in a few sled rides before school. Sarah would delight in the morning activity, laughing and screeching as Katie ran beside her barking in the crisp morning air. After several runs, a soaked Sarah would return to the house to gather her lunch and head off to school. Barbara remembers reminding her that she could wait to sled ride until after school that day. She recalls Sarah's response with a smile: "She put her little hands on her hips and replied, 'Mom, what if the sun comes out today and melts the snow?'".
—A note outside the Walden Pond gift shop

Cemetery hopping is appropriate in a state of Red Sox fans. How many times has Boston been on the verge of Heaven before crashing Harry Caray-style to diamond death? Massachusetts was an easy state for conversation starters: "So, are you a Red Sox fan?" The answerers turned pale. They paused. They thought. They grimaced. They confessed. "That must be pretty painful," I offered, commiserative balm for the damned. "Yes. Yes, it is." They looked nauseous, as though they had eaten something unpleasant. Perhaps it was swallowing the Yankees' acquisitions the previous week of David Cone and Ruben Sierra. That had to be difficult to stomach.

Rooting for the Sox (or for their National League brethren, the Cubs) is like pulling for Charlie Brown. Someday—some day—he'll kick the ball or kiss the girl. Futility cannot be eternal. But when they win they'll lose. They'll never be loved as they are now, as pained and haunted teams, because America will turn on the lovable loser-turned-winner faster than Mazeroski turned two.

America only backs the loser if he is plucky and resilient. And silent. Now that the underclasses of society are increasingly vocal, sympathy ebbs. Support is for those with the good manners to be quiet. Don't demand your turn. Wait for it. Don't push or shove. Don't dare take away what I have earned. Race remains the defining element in our culture, surpassing class and gender. Before tackling Boston's cemeteries I plotted strategy in a public library in Natick, a suburb of Boston. Natick bills itself as the Home of Champions, an odd billing considering the number of Red Sox players who have lived there.

A kind and well-meaning librarian warned me about Mattapan, where the Heavenly Twins, Hugh Duffy and Tommy McCarthy, are buried in the same cemetery. "It's bad there." I heard similar warnings in dozens of areas. In each case, "black" could have replaced bad. It's black there. The bad areas I was warned about, always, were black.

Because I was inevitably lost and needed my whereabouts affirmed more often than an insecure schoolgirl does her looks, I was forced to open my windows to some of the nation's worst areas: North Philly, East Bridgeport, East Baltimore, South Detroit, Mattapan. The Devil never entered. My frustration with race—the comments in the Deep South, the ghettoization of blacks in every major city, the weird absence of blacks at Cooperstown during the Hall-of-Fame Induction weekend (an estimated 25,000 people attended, and I saw four African-Americans)—led me to DeCordova Sculpture Park and Art Museum in Lincoln, another Boston satellite.

One DeCordova exhibit consisted of a playable 18-hole miniature golf course. The 17th hole, a par 3 titled Legacy Golf, was an indictment against those who believe three decades of affirmative action are equivalent to three centuries of negative action. A light sensor, which determined the player's color, was near the tee. "If you are a white player," read the directions, "you may choose to avoid the obstacles of the hole. This is your privilege. If you are a player of color, you have no choice but to play the entire hole making every effort to avoid its obstacles."

I chose to play as a minority, ignoring the white

hole, a large pie pan a foot from the tee. My drive was too powerful. The ball zipped past Uncle Ben's Rice Trap on each side of the fareway and sunk into the rough of the mountainous Aunt Jemima Pancake Pit. I putted out for a bird and looked more closely at the Legacy Clubhouse Trophy wall. A smiling and sweating fat white man snaked his arm around a bare-breasted African woman, who was decidedly less pleased with the relationship. The photo's caption: "Merry Christmas From South Africa. Bring 'em Back Alive. Big Game Hunter Dr. Peter Wilcox."

There was more, including a Little Black Sambo children's book and an abundance of Aunt Jemima items: cookie jar, salt and pepper sets, lights, and an odd wooden cutout, Auntie's hair wrapped neatly in a red and white bandana while a pair of baby bottle nipples poked from her chest.

As I took notes, the next players teed up. Throughout the course, the mother had cautioned her daughter about the difficult holes.

The girl, about eight-years-old, always chose the tougher route. She too played as a minority on the 17th, and parred it. Taking the tough road is the closest she'll get to real obstacles, I figured. Her path, while not set, is certainly paved to the shining pie pan. She was cute, outgoing, presumably wealthy (based on the Wellesley Softball T-shirt she wore), and white. Her legacy was set.

On the other hand, there will be problems. She'll face pressure to diet and pressure to stuff her feet into high-heels so her butt will look smaller. She'll be vulnerable when alone at night or vulnerable anytime she's with a man. She'll probably endure domestic violence at some point. Her looks will be emphasized more than her ability, the size of her breasts will be valued more highly than her SAT scores. Ask women which they'd prefer—a C cup or an A average. Or rather, ask which will get her more notice and opportunities. Maybe there should have been a third hole just for women.

Abigail Adams would have appreciated that. More than 200 years ago, not too far from where I finished my round of golf, Abigail penned a letter to husband John, who was in Philadelphia for the Continental Congress:

> *I desire you would Remember the Ladies, and be more generous and favourable to them than your ancestors. Do not put such unlimited power into the hands of Husbands. Remember all Men would be tyrants if they could. If perticuliar care and attention is not paid to the Ladies we are determined to foment a Rebellion, and will not hold ourselves bound by any Laws in which we have no voice, or Representation.*

John's thoughts were apparently on other matters, perhaps baked beans or Williams' pursuit of .400 or a sudden surge by the Yankees, because the ladies were forgotten once again.

The Adamses weren't the only noted figures in the

area. New England was loaded with them. I biked the Freedom Trail, stopping at Boston Commons where British soldiers camped at the outset of the Revolutionary War. I got a free lunch from a Food Not Bombs group. Every week they serve several hundred people, most of them homeless. My digestive system was euphoric at its reunion with vegetables.

The following day a friend and I visited Sleepy Hollow Cemetery in Concord where Thoreau, Emerson, Hawthorne, and Alcott are buried. The epitaph on Emerson's wife's stone: "The love and care for her husband and children was her first earthly interest but with overflowing compassion her heart went out to the slave, the sick and the dumb creation."

Presumably she wasn't referring to Thoreau, who was buried nearby. He loved her, the futility of which must have burned into his solitude during his years on Walden Pond. During my American Lit class in college, I read only a few of the assigned pages from *Walden*, but Thoreau became a hero nonetheless. I strove to emulate his asceticsm and reformed my spending philosophy so that it was based only on need. In 1984 I stopped buying baseball cards because I could no longer justify such purchases.

I still strive to live simply, though I feel battered by my lifestyle. Or battered by the reaction to it. My limited possessions (limited by U.S. standards but gluttonous by most of the planet's) bother many. They would rather change me—"buy some clothes, get some furniture"—than themselves. As I twice swam Walden's half-mile width, I felt I had given in. I had sold out by buying up. My possessions used to fit in my car. No longer. More clothes, a futon, VCR, much more.

The water was dazzlingly clear, almost swimming pool clear. And while my hands were easily visible beneath the surface, I knew that the vision I once had of an unemcumbered life was now submerged under a collection of things and lost focus. I sat for some time on my lawn chair, for years my lone piece of furniture, and looked out at the water.

"Beware of all enterprises that require new clothes." I laughed at the message on the shirt hanging in the Walden Pond gift store.

"It's meant to be ironic," said its creator, who worked the counter.

"Do people get the irony?" I asked.

"Oh, yes, it's our biggest seller. And it's made with organically grown cotton and non-toxic, soy-based ink. You could eat it."

You might have to. At $22 per shirt, or $2.75 per word of Thoreau wisdom (or $6 less than Thoreau spent to build his cabin in 1845), it would surely cut into a food budget.

Food remains my weakness, and I knew I should follow the advice of a second message I saw in the store. It was tucked in a back corner, explained the shirt creator, because "we don't want it too close to the big sale items."

for a man is rich in proportion to the number of things which he can afford to let alone

I left plenty alone. The pottery and stuffed

opossums, the Maine walking stick, and the Hug A Planet pillow, which promised "Vital Information For Helping Earth, From Leading Environmental Groups." Unfortunately, there were no directions on the disposal of superfluous packaging such as the cardboard frame the huggable planets arrived in. I even bypassed the $1,050 pigment transfer print.

It was more difficult to ignore the stacked copies of *Walden*. At $2 apiece, they were a bargain. I held a copy as I strolled through the store. Twice I approached the counter before returning it to the shelf.

Conway, MA   August 1, 1995

Starting with Jack Chesbro's boulder on August 1 in Conway, Massachusetts, I visited 13 graves in three days, my most prolific stretch of the trip.

Rabbit Maranville, who seemingly covered all the bases during his playing days, is doing the same in death. He is interred with his two wives in Springfield, Massachusetts. In contrast, King Kelly is buried in a lot for Elks members only. The lot, which is in Boston's Mt. Hope Cemetery, specifically excludes wives and is near the final resting place for one-time residents of the Home of Aged Women.

Boston, MA · August 3, 1995

MICHAEL J. KELLY
NOV. 6, 1894
37 YRS.

Ware, MA   August 2, 1995

Massachusetts is the burial site of 14 Hall-of-Famers, including Candy Cummings in Ware and Eddie Collins in Weston.

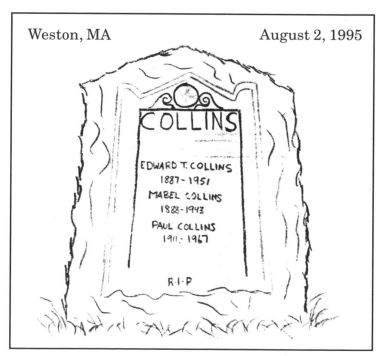

Weston, MA   August 2, 1995

Smiling Mickey Welch rests under the name of Smiling Mickey Walsh in Calvary Cemetery in Queens, New York. Willie Keeler is in the same cemetery.

27

JACKIE

The heroic cannot be the common, nor the common the heroic… Adhere to your own act, and congratulate yourself if you have done something strange and extravagent and broken the monotony of a decorous age. It was a high counsel that I once heard given to a young person, "Always do what you are afraid to do."
—Ralph Waldo Emerson

Clear-minded men of tolerance of both races realize the tragic possibilities (of integrating baseball) and have steered clear of such complications, because they realize it is to the benefit of each and also of the game.
—The Sporting News

I'm not concerned with your liking or disliking me… All I ask is that you respect me as a human being.
—Jackie Robinson

For nine years I shared a room with my older
brother. Ken was 14 and I was 10 when he began sub-
scribing to *The Sporting News*. After its arrival,
Baseball's Bible took a sacred position on our dresser
next to the most recent issue or two. They were as
prominent as Morganna's chest—and as off limits. At
that age, however, I was much more interested in staying abreast of the weekly writeups of the Giants and
Pirates and White Sox and every other team, but Ken
never allowed me to read them. Or even touch them.

Although this was long before I knew of the 8th
Amendment and restrictions against Cruel and Unusual Punishments, I knew that somehow a law was
being violated. It had to be. Not only was he withhold-
ing *The Sporting News* from his own flesh and blood,
but teasing him with it. That's sick. Following Oscar
Wilde's advice, I got rid of my temptation by yielding to
it. Surreptitiously, I would read it—the cover story,
Furman Bisher, Joe Falls, the minor league wraps,
everything—always careful not to change its position
on our dresser.

And then I awaited my punishment. Being the Big
Brother he was, he knew of my visual trespassing. I
don't know how he knew—I still don't—but he knew.
Unfortunately, he also knew a bunch of spine-twisting
holds he picked up on the high school wrestling team
and also knew that his boots had really hard tips. Ken
often tested their sturdiness against portions of my
anatomy, usually my scalp, although I seem to recall
my shins getting a fair share of attention too. I did
the requisite amount of screaming and begging and
promising never to open another issue even if McCovey

is on the cover so help me God but, for the record, I screamed and begged and promised only because I was in agony and desired to have as many brain cells as possible for puberty. If I reached it.

A good beating kept me from my fix for only a week or two. Inevitably, I'd fall and the punishment resumed. So I know about risking my life for baseball, about suffering for my love, about sacrificing my flesh to fulfill my soul, and I still didn't want to go to New York City.

During pre-trip preparations, I searched for ways to bypass it. Maybe only small towns would be on my itinerary. Baseball's rural roots and all that. Since my trip honored the past, it made no sense to go where the past is buried beneath cement, high rises, freeways, and parking garages. Or I could visit only my 100 favorite players, conveniently omitting any from the Bad Apple. But Jackie Robinson was in Brooklyn and I had to see his grave.

I knew, of course, I had to enter the city. It was my greatest fear, and to avoid it would make failures of both the trip and me. Metropolises intimidate me. Their busyness and commotion and bustle drain my confidence. But by the first week of August, my confidence was high after surviving treks into and through New York's sister cities of the Northeast: Baltimore, Philadelphia, Pittsburgh, Wilmington, Bridgeport, Hartford, and even Boston. I took on the smaller kids before I tackled the class bully.

New York City was my D-Day. There was comfort, however, in knowing mine would be easier than the original. There'd be no enfilade fire at me and from

most there'd be no language barrier. I did not anticipate peeing in my pants from fear or vomiting from
Nellie's violent lurchings. I'd see no friends explode or
acquaintances maimed or colleagues crippled.

On the night of August 6, I stared at the darkness
from my car. It was D-Day-1 and I was warm and comfortable and only slightly apprehensive. I reviewed my
battle plan. The alarm was set for 4:15 A.M. Time was
the key element to my strategy. I would leave especially early from my encampment 40 miles north of the
city. The attack would come while the city was yet
groggy or asleep, unable to counterpunch. A direct
frontal assault of New York's nightmarish morning
commute traffic would be foolish. You don't throw 85-
miles-per-hour fastballs to Stan the Man (well, maybe
now you do because he's over 70 years old). You don't
challenge what you can't beat. Like Odysseus entering
Cyclops' cave, I hoped to arrive undetected.

And once I was in, I had three maps ready for use—
one of the freeways for overall strategy, a second of
major streets for intermediate tactics, and a street map
for the anticipated fierce navigating of New York's
trenches. I was a little worried because I had been unable to study the maps closely; my eyes were still stinging from the previous day because of a chlorine overdose
in a Holiday Inn pool in Tewksbury, Massachusetts.

I scratched out a letter to my girl, or at least the
closest thing to my girl—the lesbian in Washington,
D.C.—and slept.

I awoke before the alarm and within minutes I was
on the freeway. My Silver Bullets cap was pulled low to

my forehead in the menacing, I'm-not-afraid-of-any-
thing style of Sal Maglie. Unfortunately, I felt more like
Sal Mineo. Or worse, Dal Maxvil. By 6 A.M., however, I
was parked across from Brooklyn's historic Green-
Wood Cemetery. It opened two hours later and I rushed
to find Harry Chadwick's monument, a marvelous
structure topped with a large granite ball. It sat on a

pillar with a catcher's mask and crossed bats on one side and a diamond on the others. All were bronzed and had turned green. The inscription on his grave calls him the "Father of Base Ball." Harry Wright's tomb in Bala-Cynwyd, Pennsylvania, credits him with being baseball's dad as well. I didn't have time to ponder a paternity suit or to savor Chadwick's marker. I wanted to be in and out of the city as soon as possible.

Robinson was next on the list and first among players I most respected. It has always struck me as shortsighted, or maybe just arrogant, that the 1954 *Brown vs. Topeka Board of Education* Supreme Court case, which integrated schools in theory, is viewed as the birth of the Civil Rights movement. In becoming baseball's first black player in 1947, Jackie was the anguished recipient of constant abuse. His courage and stoicism against threats, taunts, and hatred were remarkable. His success touched millions and helped the nation acknowledge the necessity of equality as much

as Rosa Parks' refusal to relinquish her seat on a Montgomery city bus eight years later. Again, why is his entrance not the starting point? Is it because sport is not a serious enough forum?

My thoughts were interrupted by a very serious but small rock. It flew though an open window and popped me on the forehead. Perhaps the city was waking up and needed to stretch and loosen its throwing arm. Blood trickled between my eyes. I drove on, dabbing my wound with a napkin as I studied my maps. The bleeding had stopped by time I reached Jackie's grave at Cypress Hills Cemetery. The grave was simple and direct. His name and a quote:

A LIFE IS NOT IMPORTANT
EXCEPT IN THE IMPACT IT HAS
ON OTHER LIVES.

A bench was part of the plot, and I sat for a long time wishing that an individual's greatness could rub off on me. I forced myself to slow down, New York City or not, and revere this man. For nearly 50 minutes I sat silently, seeing that funny way he ran, arms and legs off in contradictory directions and the Superman-like gaze, so intense, so willful. I saw the steel of his convictions and his steal of home in the World Series. Yogi screaming and steaming and stomping, Jackie heading to the dugout. I saw the racial divide that still exists in the country, but everywhere I went I also saw blacks and whites co-existing, decent people moving on from the past to bridge that divide.

And I saw myself, three months earlier, sitting on

the couch in the Oklahoma City home of a black man I had met once before. I saw myself sneaking peeks of Hideo Nomo pitching against the Pirates while my Uncle John told stories of army life and calmly mentioned his friendship and ballplaying days with Jackie. Yes, that Jackie who had been in that very same house.

Students should know about Robinson, though too many black teenage boys perceive his silence— Branch Rickey demanded he turn the other cheek during his first years in the majors—as cowardly or, at best, foolish acquiescence.

Several scraps of paper and a plastic bag lay around Jackie's marker. I picked them up and smoothed the dirt, but there was more to do. The area needed something more.

An adjacent grave had an abundance of fresh flowers. Surely no one would mind. I selected a yellow daisy, the brightest and strongest of the bunch, and laid it on Jackie's grave.

28

A PRAYER FOR MICKEY

He (Mantle) always had it in his mind that he wasn't going to make it to forty because of his uncles and his father. He really used to worry about it. We'd sit in the room and he used to talk more about that probably more than anything else. I'd say, "Goddamn it, your father and your uncles never went to the Mayo Clinic every year for a checkup, and they worked in the mines and were probably getting that stuff in their lungs all the time. You'll probably outlive us all."
—Whitey Ford

I'm forty-nine years old, that's nine years over what I ever thought I'd be. So I don't worry about it anymore.
—Mickey Mantle

Buffalo bound on Route 20, I was 70 miles west of the wonderfully named hamlet of Centerfield, New York, when I heard that Mickey Mantle was dead. It was early morning of Sunday, August 13.

My first acquaintance with Mantle came in the Miracle Mets summer of 1969 when I tore open yet another pack of baseball cards on the sidewalk beneath the orange and blue Rexall Drugs sign and saw a pale white man in a rather insincere left-handed batting stance. The back of the card was crowded with statistics, so much so that my favorite part was squeezed out. There was no room for the illustrated and insipid factoid that illuminated the player's life: "Juan Carlos played a key role in his junta's 1956 coup" or "Don's Xmas tree is one of the finest in his Pocatello, Idaho, neighborhood."

At age eight, I wasn't yet versed in reading statistics, but I could tell this man was special. The wall of numbers reminded me of the dreaded stock pages and I knew they were important. But even if I could interpret them, they would no more explain the man than 37-23-36 explained Marilyn Monroe. (It's peculiar that the two biggest icons of the 1950s had such similarly alliterative names, although many would argue that the decade's biggest and most impressive pair of icons actually belonged to Marilyn.)

Marilyn's titillating numbers only hint at her prime assets, the charisma and sex appeal. In the same way, Mickey's numbers, the 536 home runs and the 565-foot blasts, are clues to his essence, but they don't tell the full story. His power and flair cannot be understood by simple numbers. To fully comprehend the player with the mouth-watering name, you had to see the swing. He whipped the bat like a golf club and pitchers cried. And when he missed, which he often did, you felt the power as he corkscrewed into the earth, a human meltdown.

Mickey's death did not shatter me. Had my knowledge been firsthand rather than from newsreels and
books, I'd have felt differently. I'd been following his
failing health for some time and was curious about his
burial site. When I heard it would be Dallas, I was frustrated. The thought of returning to Texas, of returning
anywhere, was inconceivable. I was burning out.
Mickey would have to be part of another trip.

Since it was Sunday I decided to spend the day at
Niagara Falls and hunt up Joe McCarthy and Jimmy
Collins the next morning. I parked on the U.S. side and
biked into Canada. I figured the Falls would be
touristed out, lassoed by a cadre of exploitative busi-
nessmen, but they were too magnificent to harness.
They were too powerful. That's what they were, powerful, the most powerful thing I'd witnessed.

The Niagara River tumbled below me as though it
were the sky hurdling from the heavens while mist,

spirit-filled, floated upward, endless gifts to God. And then I knew I was wrong. God possessed even greater power. I hadn't been to church since Father's Day in Royston, Georgia, but this made up for the missed services. I stood in worshipful reverence, blessed by the music and closeness and spray of the Falls.

The area was crowded. Although it was refreshing to see ethnic diversity again, I searched for solitude. A family from Cleveland asked me for directions. They were euphoric with the Indians' success. The man knew baseball and I asked if he knew something more of Mantle.

"Mickey died? I didn't know. We listened to tapes on the way out."

He was shaken and I was sorry for my question. I rode on and stopped beside a man reading the paper. Perhaps he had information. He didn't. He was as affected as the Cleveland fan. His sadness was obvious and I felt mine coming.

Death has stayed far from me. No loved ones have died, no one I'm close to has gone. However, I worry that at some point death will pummel me for a year or two as relentlessly as the Falls. Or worse, I fear that when I'm 75, having attended dozens of funerals of friends and family, I'll still feel that no one close to me has died. I envy those who can be touched by a stranger's death. I wanted to feel that, too; I wanted to feel a part of others. I was tumbling into despair and pedaled away, straining to leave it behind.

Niagara is illuminated at night, so I squeezed into

a space at the rail and waited. The lighting was disappointing. Blues, greens, and reds muted the Falls, reminding me of an overage actress trying to hide her flaws with cheap makeup and slick lighting. Still, others were impressed, giving appropriate oohs and ahs when new colors were added. And then the ranting came from behind.

"My friends, what you see before you is nothing when compared to the power of God! If you do not accept Jesus as your personal Lord and Savior you face eternity in Hell!"

The preacher was a young, gangly man. His brown bangs tumbled across his eyes in sync with the jostled pages of his Bible as he pounded his message of love. He was part of an Ontario Bible college. With the mist spraying around him and the exaggerated motions of those who seek to hide their own lack of faith, he looked crazy. There would be no silent worship at God's altar tonight.

Two Orthhodox Jews walked by, but not unnoticed. "It doesn't matter how religious you are, without Jesus you will go to Hell!" They smiled.

And then a group of Hindus. "You who worship false gods, you will face the fires of Hell!"

I'd seen several Amish earlier in the day and hoped they would reappear. What would the preacher say to them? "You who till the land and shun materialism and practice peace and brotherhood and humility, turn to Lord Jesus or burn in Hell"?

People around me left, looking for peace from self-annointed messengers. I stayed, waiting to be approached. The leader complied. We talked and I explained his methods turned people away. I too am a Christian, and no matter how bothersome the preacher's words I saw him as family, like the buck-toothed, gravy-stained, in-desperate-need-of-a-bath cousin who shows up at weddings. Talking was futile, though. The man was so filled with God's message that he could hear no other.

I left him with his inner-turbulence and sought another spot to view the Falls. It was nice to be part of a respectful congregation, silent for the most part, in thought or reverence or awe or perhaps simply in appreciation. My silence was one of prayer. I prayed for family and for friends and for myself. And I prayed for the man who made Centerfield in New York so splendid.

29

UNTAUGHT LESSONS

*Schools do their best to fend off the intensities of
grief, the tangible realities of unjust power, and the
necessity for taking sides...Above all else they teach us
how to trim the sails of our most deep and serious
convictions, to limit the fury, to water down the passion
and to understate the pain.*
—Jonathan Kozol

"Do you have trouble finding the graves?" Alicia
asked.

Elkland Township Cemetery was to our right, and
I hoped Larry MacPhail was there. Alicia is a former
student of mine now living in Michigan. While she is
not a big baseball fan, she catches a Tigers game once
in a while and is reasonably baseball literate. Her com-
panionship had been welcome during the 90-minute
drive from Flint to Cass City.

"Sometimes there's an office or caretaker who can
provide a map or lead me directly to the grave," I

explained, as we turned onto a dirt road that led into the cemetery. "A lot of times, though, no one's there and I have to walk for an hour looking at each grave."

It looked like one of those times. There was no office in sight.

"Of course, sometimes I drive into the cemetery, look to my left, and he's right there," I joked. Now at Grave No. 93, I had long ago relinquished hope of visually stumbling upon the grave. There'd been scores of Bakers when I looked for Johnson and dozens of Johnsons when searching for McCarthy. It was never easy, and I had accepted that.

"Uh, who's the guy we're looking for again?"

"MacPhail. Larry MacPhail."

"I think we just passed him."

She was right. His marker was only a few feet down the road. Alicia, the divining rod of baseball immortals. She wandered off as I sketched the pinkish stone. No mention of his baseball exploits, only his military career.

Alicia was 50 feet away. Smoking. Blue shorts, red

T-shirt, sunglasses. Head tilted upward, she blew smoke at a 45 degree angle and looked at nothing in particular. She looked like Garbo or Bette Davis waiting for the next scene and not caring if anyone waited for her. She looked exotic, attitude and passion chiseled into her face and soul. She stood as motionless as the graves around her. Only her arm moved: cigarette to mouth and back again. Inhale, exhale, her head always at that same stony, defiant tilt.

It is a look she shows to the world, a don't-fuck-with-me look. She had it at age 16 when she ambled into my American Lit class on the first day of school in 1989. It was a brilliant class, brilliant because of its students. Five teenagers: four girls and a boy, three Guatemalans and two Americans, all bright, all opinionated, all motivated. It was a classroom of Ruth, Cobb, Grove, Paige, and Hornsby with personalities to match. Teaching is like managing—you're only as good as those you lead. When *Dead Poets Society* (*La Societa de Poetas Muertos*) opened in Guatemala, they called me Captain after the Robin Williams character. No compliment since has equalled it.

At times we were the 1950s' Dodgers. Discussions flowed. Ideas were tossed out and batted around. I never knew whether they'd turn into harmless flies or wicked line drives. We fit together so well—a perfect relay. Furillo to Robinson to Campanella. Skill. Precision. Perfection. Art. We were family,

Which also meant we were sometimes the A's of the early '70s, not the '79 Pirates. We fought and argued and debated, and that's when I first felt Alicia's look. It was usually reserved for her best friend, though I received it a number of times as well.

Alicia only spoke about the tragedy once that I can remember. I don't know what we were reading, maybe *A Catcher in the Rye*. What do you say to someone who has just had a loved one die? I asked. There was silence and that was unusual in this class. We were nervous, waiting for someone to answer. Someone, please say something.

"You can't say anything," Alicia said slowly, matter-of-factly, trance-like. There was no catch in her voice. No emotion. I don't even know if she blinked. "It doesn't change anything. It doesn't matter what you say."

Four years earlier, Alicia, age 12, went swimming in the Pacific Ocean off the coast of Champerico, a Guatemalan resort town where pigs roamed on dirty sand. The undertows were bad. She got caught. Her father rushed in to help. He too got caught. She lived. He died.

How do you survive that? How do you survive that when you're in an alien country about to face adolescence and its alien curses of teachers, parents, and hormones?

You survive by steeling yourself against the world. Early in her junior year she talked about running away. We spoke often and communicated regularly through her daily journal. I guess it's bragging to say I reached this kid, that I affected her life. Yes, the one standing over there with the smoking cigarette and smoldering personality. It's surely the greatest thing I've done.

Later that night I spoke to a girl, a high school senior, who lives with Alicia's mother and stepfather. Her voice was cold and matter-of-fact, similar to one I heard years ago. Her mother had kicked her out of the house.

"I begged her to let me come home," she said. "I didn't want to be somebody else's problem. I'm a good kid, but I make mistakes. She called me to say she was putting my cats to sleep. Then she called to say she was putting my rabbit to sleep. Then she called and said, 'Ha, ha, I bet you didn't think I'd do it.' Those animals are my family, they're my brothers and sisters. How could she do that?

"I know she has problems. There was weird stuff with her grandparents and problems with her parents. I won't be like that. I'm going to take parenting classes because I know that's part of me."

But you won't find parenting classes in many schools. You see, the answer now is back to basics. These kids, you know, what they need are the basics and the three Rs. Too much feel good, touchy-feely stuff. Why, when I was in school...

Each year dozens of damaged children float through my classes. Unable to cope with their circumstances, they do little more than survive. Teach them, I'm told. Give 'em more homework, I'm told. Look at our test scores, I'm told. America's problem is not declining SAT scores or the inability of 40 percent of our graduates to place the Civil War in the correct century. America's problem is one of the heart, not the mind. It's a problem of relationships.

How do you teach a girl about Grant and Lee and Stonewall Jackson, about Gettysburg and Appomattox Courthouse and First Manassas when there's a most Uncivil War breaking out in her home, when her mother of all people has put her siblings to sleep? What do you say to that?

It doesn't matter what you say. It doesn't change anything. You can't say anything. It won't even help to read Chapter 16 and look for answers in the back of the book.

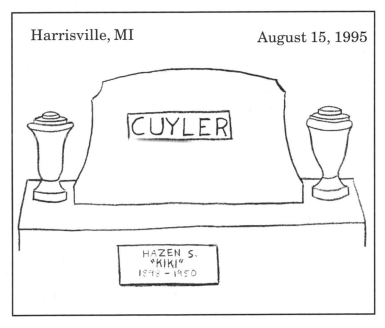

Kiki Cuyler is buried in Harrisville, Michigan, in one of the smallest cemeteries I visited.

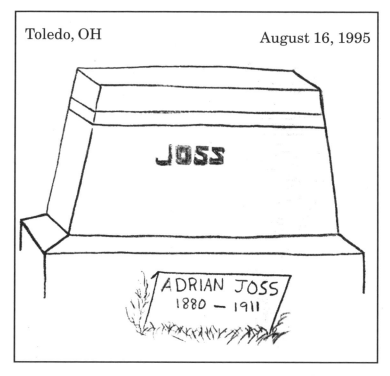

Addie Joss, meanwhile, is interred amidst Toledo's historic Woodlawn Cemetery and its 160 acres.

30

FEARFUL HOPE

*I walked all that day and into the night. As the
stars came out, I saw the constellation of Draco, high
in the northern sky. For some unknown reason this
large, curved sweep of stars gave me a sense of
hope. As I walked along, I kept looking up at it
for guidance. But with each step it became more
and more difficult to keep my eyes on the stars, for
the branches overhead grew denser and denser...
I began to wonder if I had lost my way.*
—Edward Hays

The Holiday Inn in Akron, Ohio, had no hot tub so
I moved on. Canton's didn't either so I drove another 30
miles to New Philadelphia. A hotel with just a swimming pool no longer sufficed. Indoor pools and hot tubs
are *de rigeur* for the northeast's harsh winters.
Jacuzzis had become as important as meals. With my
days filled with four to six hours of driving and perhaps
three hours in cemeteries, slipping into a hot tub late

at night was more eagerly awaited than the *Sports Illustrated* swimsuit issue at a men's college. Relaxed, I would cool off in the pool and head for Nellie where I'd been sleeping unusually well.

My lodging wasn't costing me a cent, and since an incident two weeks earlier I'd been gloating about it. After a peaceful night in Nellie I entered the hotel to shower in the exercise room. I bumped into a woman I had met the night before in the hot tub. She was furious. She hadn't slept a wink because of all that racket. Kids were running around until three in the morning and the hotel didn't do a damn thing about it and I'm paying $95 dollars a night and it damn well better not happen again. Didn't you hear anything?

Well, uh, no, I didn't but don't you think the hot tub could have been a little hotter?

I slept well in New Philadelphia and left in early morning fog on August 18 for Cy Young's hometown. The roads leading to Peoli in central Ohio were as smooth as the letter S, and my joy increased with each curve. There was little to the town, as though someone had hit the delete key to it.

Young and his right arm, which won a record 511 games in 22 years, are buried behind a Methodist Church. Presumably his left arm is there, too. The church opened its doors in 1878 when Cy was little more than a breeze and closed them in 1991 when American League Cy Young Award winner Roger Clemens won 18 games, a total Cy topped 17 times. On the other hand, Cy topped the Rocket's 10 losses on 16 occasions.

His grave was easy to find. A baseball with wings

flew above Denton and Roba-Miller Young's names. And then the epitaph:

From 1890 to 1911 "Cy" Young pitched 874 Major League Baseball games. He won 511 games, three no-hit, and one perfect game in which no man reached first base.

It seemed out of place in this small country cemetery whose paths had long ago grown over from non-use. He was the game's greatest pitcher if greatness is measured in magnitude. But it was also the ideal place, the perfect place. Mist, soft hills, farmland, silence. A postcard from the past that only the appreciative should be allowed to view.

A sign indicated fresh baked goods a mile off. The road turned to gravel and led to a cluster of homes. It was still early, not even eight, and I didn't want to wake anyone.

A man appeared, pulling a child's wagon filled with cabbage. The hat. The suspenders. Amish.

"I saw a sign about baked goods."

"Further up." He pointed toward a dirt road and disappeared.

Two dogs were screwing, blocking access to the drive. They were stuck. They strained mightily, a canine tug-of-war, their paws begged for traction. I waited. No way could I honk. Driving on Amish land already made me uneasy, like wearing muddy boots into a mosque.

The Amish are my heroes. Their lives of simplicity, principle, integrity, community, and pacifism are anachronisms in a world where the entangled pooches was as good a metaphor as any.

Pies, bread, jams, and jellies filled the backroom. The Amish woman, one of three in the kitchen, waited quietly for me to choose. They had been making shoofly pies since 4 A.M. to beat the heat. My normal banter about weather, baseball, or travel seemed silly. Three years ago I bumped into three of Mother Teresa's Sisters of Charity in an airport. We did not speak but their goodness awed me. I now felt the same.

I also felt stupid. My respect for these people is so great that I wanted them to respect me. Hey, I live simply, my car is as cheap as they come, I don't use the heater during winters, and the electric bill is usually only 10 bucks a month. I do watch TV, but just a little. A game or two of football and the news sometimes and "Frasier" and "Mad About You" and, of course, "Seinfeld." But I shower in the dark, in part to save electricity, and recycle when I can. God, I felt dirty and wasteful in their presence. Forgive me, Father, for I have sinned.

I grabbed a plate of seven cinnamon rolls and a pint of strawberry jam for $2.50. My excitement of the price stayed hidden as did the million questions I had for this living museum of a place. But I couldn't ask a single one. Let them alone. This was not a freak show, this was not Lancaster, Pennsylvania, where Cadillac-driving tourists ogle the Amish before flooding the stores, where real, honest to goodness non-Amish sell play handguns and rifles made of pine.

There was no reason to stay longer. The transaction was done and I hoped she sensed my respect. The gravel crunched beneath my tires and I anxiously munched into a roll.

It wasn't very good. Neither was the jelly.

By time I drove a mile to the church for a final look, the rolls were gone. I'd eaten them one after another and, like Indians fans for so many years, expected goodness that never came.

The church was a fitting departure point for the three-hour drive to my next grave. How much more Methodist can you get than Wesley Branch Rickey? Rickey was an oddity in his field, as much as the Amish are in society. He entered baseball when it was dominated by low-lifes, scoundrels, and rowdies. He never played ball on Sunday and was as stingy with money as he was generous with words (and with words he was downright philanthropic). Rickey, said Enos Slaughter, would "go into the vault to get you a nickel change." I couldn't help thinking that he would have approved of my thrift. On average, I was spending about $15 daily on gas, food, and lodging.

When I was a kid, I somehow came into possession of a Rickey card, raising several questions to my nine-year-old mind. What was this old guy with glasses and big eyebrows doing on a baseball card? And why did they switch his first and last names? And WHY did I end up with him when my friend got Eddie Collins? Not until my teens did I understand the significance of his signing Jackie Robinson to a Major League contract and not until much later did I begin seeing the complexities. Complexities are messy. Individuals are supposed to be either good or bad.

Rickey did not swear or drink but enjoyed a good cigar (and lots of them). In recruiting blacks to play for Brooklyn, he had part of one eye on his wallet and the rest of it on the standings. He was harsh, tyrannical, overbearing, and opportunistic. He was also good, taking one of the most courageous stands in 20th century sports. Before leaving Brooklyn to work in the Pirates' front office, Rickey received a letter from Jackie, the man he will always be linked to. The letter indicates Jackie's humility as well as Rickey's impact:

> *It has been the finest experience I have had being associated with you, and I want to thank you very much for all you have meant, not only to me and my family but to the entire country and particularly the members of our race. I am glad for your sake that I had a small part to do with the success of your efforts, and I must admit it was your constant guidance that enabled me to do so. Regardless*

*of what happens to me in the future, it
can all be placed on what you have done,
and believe me, I appreciate it....My wife
joins me in saying thank you very much,
Mr. Rickey. And we sincerely hope that we
can always be regarded as your friends
and whenever we need advice we can call
on you as usual, regardless of where we
may be.*

With a librarian's hand-drawn map, I hoped to find
Rickey's grave before a coming thunderstorm broke. A
drizzle turned harsh, and I walked blindly among the
graves trying to keep my glasses a little useful while I
fought off mosquitoes. What kind of creatures were
these, flying in the rain like this? The storm continued
and I noticed that my car windows were down. Nellie
was soaked.

A man drove up. Rickey? Right there on the edge.

An hour later I was on a bridge connecting Ohio
and Kentucky. The sun shone on the Ohio River in a
streak of dancing greens, blues, whites, and yellows. It
looked like an arrow had split the water. The day had
been long, all my days recently had been long. Was it
just this morning that I stumbled upon the Amish and
felt the peace of silent hills? Was it just this afternoon
that I crazily roamed through a mosquito-infested,
storm-pounded cemetery?

The Ohio, the dividing line of free and slave state,
rippled against its banks. Within, I felt my own rip-
pling, good and bad pounding stormlike, ricocheting in
an unseen, right-field corner between fair and foul territory. Good or bad, fair or foul. What was I?

I looked to the river for a response. Like so many
who crossed this spot last century, or who died in the
attempt, I carried the echoes of pain and hardship, of
joy and laughter, into a future I understood only as
fearful hope. I carried these things because I had to. I
was alone.

31

SMOKING HEROES

The choices we make are ultimately
our responsibility.
—Eleanor Roosevelt

The woman at the desk was a couple of hundred pages into *Gone With the Wind*. I eyed the three security screens suspiciously and wondered if somewhere someone was doing the same to me. I was in Eastern Kentucky University's Earle Combs Residence Hall. How many colleges have all-women's dorms named after left-handed center fielders with lots of speed and no power?

Combs played for the Yankees from 1924-1935 and was elected to the Hall of Fame in 1970. I knew that because I'd gone to his grave earlier that day in Richmond City Cemetery. Actually, it was more of a monument, a monument surrounded by the small, rectangular, unobtrusive headstones of his relations, including one for Earle, Jr. The monument was disturbing.

Sure, go ahead and mention you're in the Hall but no
need to shout it megaphone-like among the dead.
There is no need to acknowledge fame so vociferously.
Surely the locals knew who he was.

Or did they?

After a dinner at Fat Fred's—all the slaw, mashed potatoes, greens, corn muffins, white beans, and railroad tie-sized fries you can eat for $3.50—I stopped at Combs Hall. It is one of three all-women dorms on campus. Three years ago there was only one, the woman at the desk told me. She was a senior sociology major. Her reading interrupted, I mentioned that Scarlet's toughness made her one of my favorite literary characters— how would Scarlet fare housed only with females? —and asked what she thought of the Shannon Faulkner situation.

"I don't know who she is."

Faulkner had left the Citadel the day before, ending her fight to join the men-only military school that trains South Carolina's elite as well as its misogynists. If this woman was unaware of Faulkner, it was unlikely anyone would be familiar with Combs. It was Saturday night, a little before seven, so there was no shortage of activity. Men were not allowed in women's rooms without signing in at the desk and showing identification. Most called upstairs from the lobby and waited. They acknowledged me respectfully as though I were their date's father.

I approached them and explained that I was doing research on Combs and asked if they knew who he was. If they didn't, I asked them to make a guess. They looked scared, like I had asked them out for a bowl of grease with extra cholesterol at Fat Fred's. Usually with prodding and encouragement, they answered. The responses:

—Wasn't he a baseball player?
—Former president of university.
—One of the founders.
—Football coach.
—He did something in Kentucky. I know,
   he was governor.
—Professor of Math
—Professor of Gardening.
—An architect, but looking at this building
   I doubt that.
—A really old teacher of history.
—He made great sociological advances.
—He was a Doctor of Philosophy.
—He invented Honey Combs.
—Teacher of English.
—He killed himself here.
—President of the University.
—An artist. In sculpture.
—Heart surgeon.
—Financial administrator.
—He was a politician, a senator from Kentucky.
—He built skyscrapers.
—Brain doctor.

A near leadoff single followed by 20 consecutive
whiffs, bloops, and comebackers.

The parade of couples through the lobby disturbed
me. Why wasn't I in a relationship? And why hadn't
some woman tried to hit on me? This had become an
obsession in recent weeks. It was August 19, my 116th
day on the road. I'd been in 32 states, driven 17,000

miles, fallen for a lesbian, and been attacked by a
mute. Odds are that some woman would have made a
move. Geez, even the '62 Mets won 40 games. But no
woman had singled me out for her affections. No des-
perate divorcees or demure librarians or undersexed
divas (or oversexed ones for that matter). No cemetery
secretaries. No wanton women with passion to spare.
No homely homemakers or drunk co-eds. If I were fishing, my hook would be adrift without a nibble.

I was more befuddled than upset.

It was still early and still warm so I returned to the
Holiday Inn and swam. I was exhausted but rarely
retired to the parking lot before 11. Most activity had
subsided by then, as had the heat and risk of someone
peeking in the back window as I slept. I sat in the lobby
and updated my journal.

A man sat beside me. Normally I would have initi-
ated a conversation; tonight, I just wanted to write.
For one of the few times on the trip someone else spoke
first. People are starved for conversation. Most, unfortunately, are afraid. Too much risk. They'll comment
on a baby or a pet because those are safe topics, bridg-
ing the loneliness of one shore with the awkwardness
of another.

He was friendly, about 50, maybe older. Joe. He was
interested in my doings and I asked about his.

"I'm a tobacco buyer for RJ Reynolds and grow a
little tobacco myself." During the drive from Ports-
mouth to Richmond and later to Pisgah for Happy
Chandler's grave, I'd seen fields of strange yellow
plants that reminded me of lethal pod-producers from
a sci-fi movie. When I saw the leaves hanging and

drying in barns, I knew I wasn't far off. My contempt for anyone connected with tobacco was total.

Funny, but Joe didn't look like Satan's agent. Where do you buy from, what region?

"Mostly in Pennsylvania. From the Amish."

"The Amish!" I didn't mean to shout. "The Amish sell tobacco?"

"Yes, they do. They don't smoke it, though, just one cigar on the day of sale."

By our 30s, we should be jaded and cynical, immune to fallen heroes, suspicious of our saints. But this was huge. This was Mother Teresa overseeing a sweatshop. This was Cesar Chavez sneaking off for a burger during a fast. This was Thoreau having a Shop 'Til You Drop sign on his mantle. This was corked bats and illegal pitches. This was Jackson and Weaver and Cicotte and the rest of the Black Sox dumping the 1919 World Series. God, no, not the Amish. Say it ain't so, Joe.

"Do you feel bad about growing something that's so harmful?" I asked.

He paused. "Yeah, I think about it. I feel bad sometimes. I wouldn't want my children to smoke."

"Then why grow it?"

"Name something that's grown that isn't harmful."

"Broccoli."

"It's harmful to me. I grew it one year and lost 30 thousand dollars."

We laughed hard. When he left a pair of charred images remained. No longer were the Amish the pure, idyllic, wholesome, dignified community. And no longer could I view the tobacco grower as a straw-in-the-mouth, shit-in-the-ear, heart-in-the-wallet hick (or as a slick-thinking, amoral executive whose idea of compassion is a final smoke with a colleague dying of lung cancer).

They were closer than seemed possible. I still revere the Amish for their virtues. It's too bad, though, that in this one area that kills millions they are no different from the likable small-town farmer or the unapproachable big-time C.E.O. It's too bad that when it comes to tobacco the Amish, frankly, don't give a damn.

THE LEGEND

(A Parable)

My assumption is that the story of any one of us is
in some measure the story of us all.
—Friedrich Buechner

I don't know when the blister started. It was on the finger of my drawing hand, and every time I drew I was in agony. Perhaps I'd been overdoing it. When I arrived at Bethel Cemetery in Phillipsburg, Ohio, for Jesse "Pop" Haines' grave on August 21, I'd already made stops that day for Miller Huggins, Waite Hoyt, Eppa Rixey, Buck Ewing, and Walter Alston.

The Cardinal righthander's grave was odd. (Whadda ya expect from a knuckleballer? cynics might whine.) Jesse and wife Carrie's names were on beveled sections raised on each end of a rectangular block. A cylinder rose in the middle and at its top was a sundial with a pair of cardinals, each gripping a bat, an hour

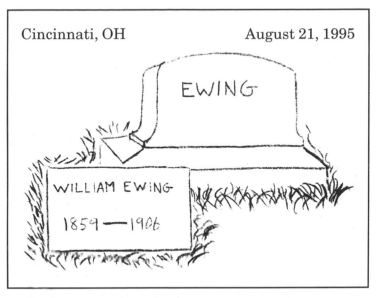

Cincinnati, OH   August 21, 1995

glass with wings, and information on St. Louis' pennant- and World Series-winning teams.

Drawing it was daunting; I doubted I could do it, especially with a bad digit. Despite my wariness and injury I had to try.

Wind roared through the surrounding cornfields. In the distance, an old ranchhand sat. A bull circled restlessly about him but he appeared unphased. He may have been asleep.

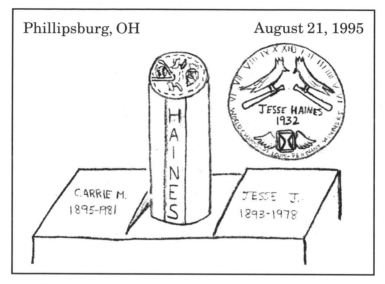

Phillipsburg, OH   August 21, 1995

HAINES

JESSE HAINES
1932

CARRIE M.
1895-1981

JESSE J.
1893-1978

The cemetery caretaker approached me. "Who's that?" I asked, motioning toward the man.

"Who? Ol' Pete? Best hand around here. Looks to me like he's gettin' off a drunk. But he deserved it. Corralled the toughest group you'll ever wanna see yesterday. Queer fella but they don't come any better."

My first lines were tentative, shallow attempts at drawing. The pain slowly lessened and confidence increased as the foundation took shape. Perhaps I could do it. The base was set, as were Carrie's and Jesse's names. I began working on the cylinder. This was the heart of the grave, its power.

It was formidable, and the top required a particularly fine touch. Otherwise all my effort would go for naught.

The cylinder's base and top were way off. I had lost my ability to show depth. Everything was wrong. And then I noticed the pencil, smeared with blood. I rose from my chair and kicked the patch of dirt below. The corn waved and screamed frantically. Sweet Jesus, it looked alive.

The caretaker had been observing my work from a distance. He came near, looked at my finger, and spat. "That's enough, kid, you did good."

He looked toward Pete and called. I still don't know how Pete heard anything over the roar of the corn and wind. He got up, tiredly, and walked toward us, the longest, slowest walk I've ever seen. He looked old. He was old. The graying hair, the leathery face. Too many summers in this damn sun.

The caretaker handed Pete my book and pencil and explained the situation. "Can you do it?"

Two of Indiana's six Hall-of-Fame graves: Stanley Coveleski in South Bend and Edd Roush in Oakland City.

"We'll see."

Pete drew a few practice lines, really just absent-minded doodling. He was ready. Even from several feet away, the concentration was obvious. He looked like a surgeon with an X-ray deciding where to begin.

Three strokes later he had the cylinder. Amazing. But he still had the top, he wasn't out of this yet. He was so careful and methodical. Each line had purpose. No wasted energy. The cardinals and bats, the numbers and words, the hourglass encased by bats, they all appeared, creations of God. His work, his masterpiece, was complete. He had indeed saved me.

Years later I heard that Pete continued his artistry only a while longer. He bummed around, never able to kick the demon liquor he loved so much. His town scorned him. Many say he threw away his life, that you can't drink and draw and expect to live. Maybe so. But that doesn't explain this picture in my mind, this picture of Ol' Pete strolling from the bullpen on that wonderful, warm Ohio day. It doesn't explain why that picture will never die.

William Hulbert's unique marker in Graceland Cemetery in Chicago. The ball lists the National League teams during Hulbert's stint as president: Boston, Providence, Worcester, Troy, Chicago, Cleveland, Buffalo, and Detroit.

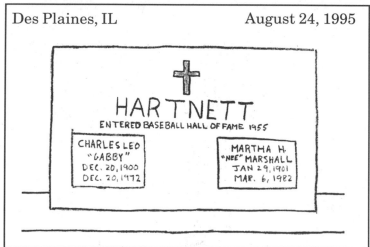

Des Plaines, IL   August 24, 1995

HARTNETT
ENTERED BASEBALL HALL OF FAME 1955

CHARLES LEO
"GABBY"
DEC. 20, 1900
DEC. 20, 1972

MARTHA H.
"NEE" MARSHALL
JAN 29, 1901
MAR. 6, 1982

Rube Foster and Gabby Hartnett are two of the 10 Hall-of-Famers buried in the Chicago area. Hartnett died on his 72nd birthday.

Charles Comiskey's crypt in Evanston, Illinois.

33

CAP'S EVIL GAME

I was a natural born kicker bent upon
making trouble for others.
—Cap Anson

At 5'4" and 145 pounds, Wee Willie was small, even smaller than Little Napoleon and Little Poison, who was the little brother of Big Poison but not related at all to Big D, Big Six, Big Train, or the Big Cat.

The Big Cat no doubt would have intimidated Goose, Chick, Ducky, and Rabbit. He'd have a considerably tougher time with Crab, the Gray Eagle, Beauty and the Beast, the Iron Horse, and especially the Iron Man.

As strange as it may seem, the Iron Man was not connected at all—not by solder or rivets or bolts—to the Mechanical Man. Far from a robot, the Mechanical Man was as literate as he was alliterate. The same could be said for Hustlin' Hugh, Hammerin' Hank, Gorgeous George, Gentle Jeems, the Fordham Flash,

Mighty Mite, Master Melvin, King Kelly, King Carl, the Commerce Comet, the Kentucky Colonel, or the Tall Tactician, who by the end of his days should have been known as the Ancient Tactician. He was 88 when he left baseball.

That was old, older than Foxy Grandpa. Older too than Ol' Eagle Eye and Ol' Stubblebeard, as well as Old Hoss, the Old Roman, and Old Aches & Pains (who can't be blamed for having a few). He was even older than the Old Professor, who was a pretty good source of advice, better than any Rube or Schoolboy and on par with his old (of course) pal, Uncle Robbie. If you weren't satisfied with them you could appeal to a higher authority, including Chief, the General, Sir Timothy, Earl of Snohomish, Duke of Tralee, Knight of Kennett Square, the Sultan of Swat, the Deacon, the Rajah, or the Mahatma.

The Mahatma shouldn't be confused with Gandhi, that Fastin' Indian, or, for that matter, with Smilin' Mickey, Happy Jack, Slidin' Billy, the Flying Dutchman, Bucketfoot Al, Sunny Jim, Orator Jim, Black Mike, Wahoo Sam, Gettysburg Eddie, Memphis Bill, Georgia Peach, Hoosier Thunderbolt, Cool Papa, or Three-Finger Brown.

Commenting on an individual's traits was once common, as common as the nose on your face. Just ask Schnozz. Or Cocky, Catfish, or Kiki, who as a stutterer might have a tough time responding. Gabby wouldn't, nor Dizzy, certainly not The Lip, and we can only guess about Pud, Pie, Cracker, and Candy.

Happy would be, well, happy to tell you a thing or three. So would Goofy, including the fact that he also went by Lefty, a great baseball moniker, right up there with Bucky, Buck, Hack, Kid, Red, Pep, Pop, and, to top it all off, Cap.

Cap.

Cap Anson.

What a beautiful, sweet-day, blue-sky, green-grass, let's-play-two, isn't-America-great name. As a kid (not Nichols), I loved that name. Short, sweet, starting authoritatively—the hard C, the pop of the P—and ending gracefully, Anson sliding off the tongue. His stroke was just as authoritative and graceful. And he had the stats to give his name meaning. What a hitter. What a player.

What a racist.

A large monument was at his gravesite in Oak-Woods Cemetery in Chicago. The monument was striking. The middle column had a garland bracketing a ball and crossed bats above the inscription:

CAPT. ADRIAN CONSTANTINE ANSON
BORN AT MARSHALLTOWN, IOWA, APRIL 15, 1852
DIED AT CHICAGO, APRIL 14, 1922
HE PLAYED THE GAME
ERECTED TO HIS MEMORY BY THE NATIONAL LEAGUE
OF PROFESSIONAL BASE BALL CLUBS

Yes, he played the game, but a hell of a lot of others did not and he's as much to blame as anyone. Anson was the preeminent player of 19th century baseball. He was to the game then what Frank Thomas or Griffey is to it now, only he had clout off the field, too.

In 1886, Anson was among the league leaders in hitting, slugging, hits, doubles, home runs, total bases,

and RBI. A year later, his totals were down slightly, although he was still among the league's best players. *The Baseball Encyclopedia* credits him with 18 strikeouts, though that is one too few, for on July 19, 1887, Cap Anson, first baseman, manager, pride of Marshalltown, Iowa, faced the toughest of opponents: history, tradition, and peer pressure. By refusing to play Newark, an integrated team that featured a

Canadian black pitcher named George Stovey, Anson
fanned in the moral department. Stovey feigned stomach problems and removed himself from the lineup so
the game could be played. It was a mistake on par with
giving in to terrorists. Anson had his way with Newark
and within two years would have his way with the
other professional clubs.

Anson was among the league leaders in ousting
blacks from organized baseball, or base ball as it was
referred to at the time. He did, however, have contact
with at least one black, an entertainer named Clarence
Duvall, who served as mascot of Anson's Chicago White
Stockings.

Anson's disdain toward blacks was odd. He can't be
called a product of his environment. He was no Southerner; he was born in Iowa. And why such acquiescence
to his purge? To be sure, Anson was a powerful man, a
leader, a force, but there were many powerful men in
the game in the six decades between Stovey's stomach-
ache and Rickey's signing of Jackie Robinson. At least
one of those men could have stood up. Where was
McGraw with his secret list of Negro Leaguers he coveted? Where was the dignified Mr. Mack, speaking of
righteousness and oozing integrity? Where was
Mathewson or Johnson or Ruth, idols who could have
turned the tide of segregation?

And where was Commissioner Landis? He, too, is
buried at Oak-Woods. No grave fit its corpse so well.
The marker was stone, the engraving stern and
austere, all lines and corners and edges. There was
nothing soft about it or the man who banned Joe Jackson and seven others from baseball for life for conduct
harmful to the game. So Shoeless Joe helped throw the

1919 Series. Is that any more harmful than leading the ouster of blacks from baseball and, once they were out, making sure they stayed out?

And if the concern is conduct harmful to baseball, we shouldn't stop with an illiterate, hoodwinked, South Carolina farmboy who outperformed nearly every player on each team. What about players who renegotiate fat contracts, who skip to another team because $4 million makes ends meet better than $3.2 million? What about the strike? What about canceling six weeks of the most statistically interesting season in recent years? What about flipping off fans or not running out grounders? Or spitting on umpires? Or calling off the World Series? That's not harmful?

If moral fiber is such a great concern, then let's take a closer look at who's in the Hall of Fame. Maybe it should take something more than great stats and a cool nickname.

34

BATS AND
(WEDDING) BELLS

*Very few players are ever as valuable to a team
the first year they're married as they are before or
after...I have known young bridegrooms, on the
bench, to forget whether there were men on base or
not. They are thinking about that new apartment,
about that new furniture, that fancy gas range, and
so on. It is a beautiful state of bliss, but, take it from
me, a young man in that state of mind doesn't win
many ball games...These foolish wives or sweet-
hearts who sit in the stands and yell out endearing
encouragement to their husbands are a genuine
distraction...You can well imagine the feelings of a
player when he leaves the bench to go to bat at a
critical moment and suddenly hears a soprano voice
from the stands: "There goes my dearie!"*
—John McGraw

En route to meeting my future wife in Minneapolis, I stopped at a Holiday Inn in Beloit, Wisconsin. First impressions being what they are, I wanted to clean up. The lobby was empty except for a youngish, blond woman at the desk. I acted as though I belonged in the hotel and, in my search for a swimming pool to bathe, ignored her as I walked past.

"Hey, Pretty Boy."

Finally. After 19,000 miles (actually, it was only 18,719), a woman, a female, a member of the opposite sex, was hitting on me. I turned toward her with my best shy smile and twinkling, oh-are-you-talking-to-me? eyes. She wasn't. She stared toward a cage several feet away and made insipid faces to a parrot.

Cary (named after Cary Grant) had to be an improvement. A friend had met her a few days before my departure in April and felt we were destined to wed. Although I had thought of her little during the trip, meeting my bride-to-be would be a prudent move. Usually I am an overwhelmed rookie when meeting women, but I was too tired to be nervous. I knocked and waited.

She bounded toward the door, and I was surprised by her height.

She's a 7-footer—if you count the two she walks on—and explodes into life, perhaps the result of her Italian and Greek bloodline. We talked about my sojourn of gravesites. She wasn't contemptuous, a good sign. We ate dinner at a Lebanese restaurant, talked until it closed, and then went to a waterfall, beautiful at night.

I left early the next morning, wondering if I should have kissed her. I had in my dream. The day's trip would be long—about seven hours of driving for two graves in Wisconsin—but I thought it symbolic that I was off to see Beauty Bancroft in Superior. My second stop would be in Clear Lake for Burleigh Grimes, Ol' Stubblebeard, the last legal spitballer. John Kiernan wrote that Grimes "always looked like a man who was about to commit assault and battery when he threw the ball." I tried to ignore the symbolism in that.

My dark hair and features stood out in the Scandinavian town of Clear Lake as much as my California plates, but I didn't feel like a stranger as I often did in other small cities. I sought directions to the cemetery. Two old women, when informed of my objective, exclaimed that it was too bad Charles Clark was away on business. "He knows everything about Burleigh," said one.

"Wait, there he is now," said the other, pointing to the silver-haired, somewhat portly Clark. He is a city councilman; recently Clear Lake's newspaper folded, so he started one—not for today's residents, he said, but "to preserve history."

Clark has done the same for Grimes' past. The two were neighbors, friends, and as close as the best of families. Between greetings with fellow residents, Clark offered me a 10-minute tour of his home and then a trip to the cemetery. I consented reluctantly. I was more interested in a quick sketch of the grave and a return trip to see Cary.

A baseball weathervane topped his home, which had a street address of 1954. That was Cleveland's last time in the Series, Clark pointed out. Inside there was more baseball. Photos covered the walls. Clark with Williams. With Williams and Feller. With Palmer. With Killebrew. Several pictures of Burleigh. With Rachel Robinson, Jackie's wife. "I'm really proud of that one. What a gracious woman."

Then the memorabilia, ranging from priceless to arcane to bizarre. Grimes' St. Louis Cardinals World Series ring. ("Charley, I want you to have this," Burleigh told Clark at a holiday dinner.) A lamp—its base a bronzed mitt—and Burleigh's glove from Game 7 of the 1931 Series which he pitched and won. The stand was composed of three sections of a sawed-off Babe Herman bat. I half expected the shade to be made of Creepy Crespi's uniform. Or skin.

A license plate was in the corner: BAG 270. Ol' Stubblebeard's initials and win total. Clark then showed me a bat, Burleigh's bat, that compiled a .248 average (.316 in 19 Series at-bats).

I reached for it. Clark held it tight, off on another

story. Every item had a story and Clark was the narrator.

"Burleigh was a good-hitting pitcher, you know. He always said, 'You got to do the little extra things—hit, field—if you want to stay around.'"

I wanted—I needed—to hold the bat, but Clark was off on another anecdote, something about Feller. Bats have always fascinated me. In Little League I used a 29-inch Reggie Jackson Adirondack model. It made five appearances against Mark Langston, now of the Angels. He struck me out twice before I dribbled a seeing-eye single to right. (Hey, it's a line drive in the boxscore!) Mark was so thrilled to yield a hit to his classmate and friend that he drilled me on the knee my next two at bats. The ball's seams were still visible on my flesh a few days later as I helped Mark through World History.

During the season I slept with my bat. I hope that's not strange or some sort of phallic hang up. I hope it's just another part of normal adolescent male development, like making your little sister's life miserable and talking to baseball cards, which I also did. I once kissed my bat after a Hornsby-esque round of batting practice, but mocking teammates stopped me of that habit.

A solid hit, the kind that echoes through the stands and your body, is one of the purest of actions. At a Lookouts game in Chattanooga two months earlier, a local documentary producer took his British girlfriend to her first baseball game. She was beyond ignorant. Her first question was, "What's an out?" We alternated explanations of various facets of the game, but he was the one to talk about hitting; it was his girlfriend, after all. He explained that a good hit is better than an orgasm. I've heard other men say the same, which makes me wonder a couple of things. First, what do women compare sex to? And second, maybe this whole bat thing *is* phallic. Swinging a bat, even now, even an imaginary one, creates a solid, in control, I-can-do-anything, all-is-right-with-the-world feel. How often does sex do that?

Clark handed me the bat. Reluctantly. He stayed near. Was he afraid I would drop it?

He needn't have worried. My grip was sure, my forearms bulged, as much as forearms can after four months of driving atrophy. I imagined stepping in against Hubbell, Root, Vance, Dizzy, Grover, Koufax. I was lost in the game's past.

I envied Clark, and admired him. His friendship with Burleigh opened doors to seemingly all the greats of the last 60 years. He is a collector of memorabilia for love of the game, not for money. The room is for those who cherish baseball.

"Here, take this," he said. "You've come such a long way."

Burleigh's autograph.

Burleigh used to sign for everyone, Clark explained. He'd sit on his porch and sign balls and letters and send them back. "You can't just take from the game," Burleigh used to say, "you got to give something back."

My 10-minute tour had turned into an hour. As much as I enjoyed the bat, I was anxious to see Cary again. She was softer than a Louisville Slugger and just as sweet. Second impressions being what they are, I stopped at a county office building to shave and clean up. I was 20 miles away when I realized I had left my Silver Bullets cap in the bathroom. It had become a big part of the trip and its sentimental value was already immense. It was increasingly battered, which made it even better as a keepsake. I backtracked but it was gone. I felt sick, and hated whomever took it. I was angry at myself too. Why had I let a woman I'd just met make me concerned about my appearance?

The anger was mostly gone when I saw Cary that afternoon. It was forgotten by evening when we created a faux wedding invitation for my matchmaker friend. The reception is slated at the Field of Dreams, according to the invitation, while the "blissful couple will be registered at Bloomingdale's and the Hall of Fame Gift Shop."

I hope they sell bats.

35

HEADING HOME

It is designed to break your heart. The game begins in the spring, when everything else begins again, and it blossoms in the summer, filling the afternoons and evenings, and then as soon as the chill rains come, it stops and leaves you to face the fall alone.
—A. Bartlett Giamatti

I left Minneapolis and Cary on Tuesday, September 5, at 7:30 P.M, debating if I should have invited her along for the final stages, which mainly consisted of a sprint to the West Coast. My goal was to reach Olympia, Washington, by early Saturday. I had friends there. The 9th was my 35th birthday and I did not want to spend it alone on the road.

Only small pieces remain from that 2,000-mile stretch, including a 645-mile marathon from Rapid City, South Dakota, to Butte, Montana, on September 7. I remember stopping at Little Big Horn, eating bull testicles in western Montana ("I Had A Ball At The Testicle Festival," reads my refrigerator magnet), and wearing my U.S. Secret Service cap and CCCP Baseball shirt (complete with hammer and sickle) in the Idaho panhandle in hopes of tweaking some of the antigovernment, commuphobes nesting there.

What I remember most was the horror of seeing a white Grand Prix with California plates in South Dakota heading west on I-90. An old woman drove and I knew my odyssey was ending. It'd been more than three months since I'd last seen a car from my home state. Nellie and I had stood out in our travels and now we would again be commonplace. Another car and man in a region teeming with them. For only a short while longer would I capture the attention and fascination of strangers with explanations of my quest. For months I had the freedom of a child pouncing on a king-size bed in his hotel room, but there was a knock on the door and I would have to stop my play to answer it.

Routine, with its paralysis and short-sightedness and dream-killing tendencies, would once more be upon me, and I knew I wouldn't handle it well. I am unique and special and wanted to be treated as such. Routine doesn't allow that. It does, however, permit stability and stability allows relationship. But relationships are struggles; it is easier to be alone. So I fought the desire to be lost, even forgotten in this country. The thought of routine and relationship is so scary that I often drive the emotional equivalent of a bumper car, occasionally in contact with others, but more often swerving, sideswiping, dodging, dashing, darting, veering, anything to avoid solid contact, to avoid moments of silent love when the next word or look will send me reeling out of control, stripping me naked, exposing inadequacies, fears, and everything else we cover with a brave front to survive the unspoken agony of daily life. The demons that started the trip had been silent for weeks—fried in Baltimore's heat? steamrolled in New York's traffic?—but their offspring were just as tenacious and vocal.

I awoke at 4:45 A.M. in Ellensburg, Washington, on my birthday and drove the remaining 175 miles through spectacular forest en route to Olympia. Friends Jim, Penny, and Diana celebrated my arrival. Diana in particular unleashes enthusiasm and love like warm blankets to the homeless; I felt special. This would be one of the last times I would stay with friends. They had made the trip possible, providing much more than the necessities. They were fueling stations of faith, funneling belief in my dream when belief ebbed.

Curiously, my stops with friends had alternated on
a liberal-conservative basis the entire trip. A
Reaganite would be followed by a socialist, staunch
pro-lifers by fierce pro-choicers, homophobes by homo-
sexuals, lovers of Limbaugh by adamant feminists,
born again Christians by agnostics. They were all
people of principle and strong belief and I increasingly
sensed my fortune to know them.

While stopped at a light in Seattle, only a few miles
from Amos Rusie's grave, I was rear-ended by a postal
worker and stayed an extra day in Olympia. Nellie suf-
fered minor injuries, including a broken tail light, and
my back tightened like a rookie in a pennant race. I
waited anxiously in a hospital emergency room while
Diana snapped photos of me in a wheelchair and neck
brace. I was healthy enough to travel the following day.
Too close to be sidelined, I drove 572 miles to Klamath
Falls, Oregon, and slept in Nellie for the final time.

I had been to Eagleville Cemetery before. It looked
the same—the small, grassless graveyard with the
magnificent Warner Mountains as a backdrop. This
time I hoped to find Arky.

On Memorial Day weekend in 1994 I opted to do a
trial run of grave-searching. I selected Alturas, California, in the state's northeastern corner, a day's drive
from the Bay Area. Arky Vaughan, the brilliant Pirate
and Dodger shortstop, was supposed to be buried there.
He was only 40 when he died in 1952 trying to save a
friend from drowning in nearby Eagle Lake.

As I prepared for the trip, I was still mourning my
parents' separation. A month earlier they had decided
that 28 years of marriage was enough, or maybe that it
was too much. I had been feeling sorry for myself,
spending cold evenings at the Oakland Coliseum,
where I sat in fractured solitude, watching the pitiful
A's and ingesting Jumbo Jack tacos by the half-dozen.
On the morning of that first visit to Alturas, I was
blasted awake at 3:11 by music from my $2 clock radio.
"DON'T YOU CRY NO MORE" was the opening salvo.
Kansas (or was it God?) told me to carry on, promising
that peace would replace confusion.

That morning's alarm was a wakeup call in more
ways than one. Slowly—and isn't that always the
case?—I had become complacent, watching another
round of "Cheers," hiding misery, concealing it with the
moderate and mundane. My life had become boring.
But sacrifice and life happens. But then it is no sacrifice at all because you have gained so much.

I overlooked Arky the first time, but not the second.
The early morning warmth was ideal as I sketched. I
studied the harsh, dry beauty around me before returning to Nellie. It was unlikely I'd be this way again
and I wanted to preserve the sight. I needed one last
look before I headed home.

36

INVINCIBILITY

There comes a time in every man's life and I've
had plenty of them.
—Casey Stengel

I guess I'm like the venerable old warrior Chief
of the Great Six Nations, who announced his
retirement by saying, "I am like an old hemlock.
My head is still high, but the winds of close to a
hundred winters have whistled through my
branches, and I have been witness to many wondrous
and many tragic things. My eyes perceive the
present, but my roots are embedded deeply
in the grandeur of the past."
—Chief Myers

My mind was already playing tricks on me. It was
September 26 and beyond my grasp that exactly five
months earlier I had left San Leandro to begin my journey. Was I ever concerned about finishing? The doubts

and fears, they weren't real, were they? Before I began my final day of travel, I checked my boxscore—my journal—to know they were.

Driving north on Highway 101, the San Francisco Bay on my right, Candlestick Park emerged. It is a landmark for me, a concrete spaceship structure that holds excitement, memories, and, once in a while, a good team. How is it that the first day I ever spent there remains the most vivid? I was eight and Mom and Dad let my brother Ken, my best friend Rick, and me take the bus to see the Giants play a doubleheader against the Mets. A man next to me wondered if this Bobby Etheridge kid might be the Giants' third baseman of the future. He wasn't. He never played another season in the majors.

It was August 1969 and, I have to say it, a perfect day for baseball. Candlestick was not enclosed then and you could still see the Bay beyond right field. We sat in the bleachers and I watched a young Bobby Bonds play catch with Willie McCovey. We had binoculars, but they were unnecessary because every player was already larger than life. I swear I heard McCovey's throws snap into Bonds' glove. Adult logic tells me that is impossible, but I will always hear it; I will always believe it.

The Mets were making their amazing run for the division title, and 24-year-old Tom Seaver helped them along in the opener. He shut down the Giants and nearly killed Ron Hunt. A Seaver fastball drilled Hunt in the head and ricocheted several rows beyond the protective screen behind homeplate. Hunt lay motionless and was removed on a stretcher.

The nightcap went extra innings. Bonds stopped
the go-ahead run with a spectacular throw for an 8-2
double play. San Francisco won in the 10th when a
ready-to-retire Jim Davenport walked with the bases
loaded. I've often considered researching those games
to see who played. Did Nolan Ryan pitch or Koosman or
McGraw? How'd McCovey do, and did Mays get in the
game? But I'm afraid that some of my images are false.
Maybe there was no great, game-saving throw from
deep center. Maybe there was no nearly decapitated
second baseman or fortuitous base on balls. Maybe
childhood memories, distorted, misshapen, even wrong,
are a truth that should be sheltered and nurtured.
Sometimes it's best to let the mind work its magic.

There is ongoing talk of a new park for the Giants.
I hope it fails. Candlestick is home. The wind and cold,
which receive more verbal abuse than the hated Dodgers, are part of its charm. The climate adds character to
the park as much as the ivy in Wrigley or the Green
Monster in Fenway or the Milwaukee knucklehead
who slides into a giant glass of beer after a Brewer
home run.

The Giants' 1995 season died long before I drove
past the park. If there were a headstone, though, you'd
find it in Colma. Just south of San Francisco, Colma has
17 cemeteries. San Francisco banned burials within city
limits in the early 1900s because real estate was too
valuable. The city began exhuming bodies and rebury-
ing them in Colma, a project that lasted until 1941.

I passed a pet cemetery on my way to Holy Cross
Cemetery. I'd been amused to see on my Hall-of-Fame
list that Holy Cross was the burial site for both George

Kell and George Kelly. The secretary found Kelly easily, but had no record of Kell. This was not unusual so I double-checked his death date on my list. It was the same as Kelly's. That couldn't be, and then I remembered. George Kell was at Cooperstown for the Induction ceremonies. He was selling his autograph, which isn't bad for a dead man.

There were no deceased Tigers at Pet's Rest, although cheetahs have been buried there, as well as dogs, cats, monkeys, and goldfish. More than 13,000 animals have been interred in the cemetery since its founding in 1947. I came across a Mickey and a Duke but saw no reference to the Bay Area's greatest player. How difficult could it be to correct that?

"This is very hard for me," I told the manager, my voice soft and pained. "My wife and I, our cat, it was my wedding gift to her, it died....Forgive me, but it's been very difficult."

"I'm so sorry. What kind of cat was it?"

This caught me by surprise. I know little about

cats other than they annoy the hell out of me. My mind raced, searching madly for types of cats. I knew of only one.

"Siamese."

"How big?"

How big? If your Uncle Wilbert dies you don't ask how big he was. How am I supposed to know how big. I put my hands 18 inches apart and asked about burial costs. It depends on what type of plaque and what you have engraved, he told me.

"Can I have 'Say Hey' put on it, and maybe even a baseball? Her name was Say Hey in honor of Willie Mays."

As I drove into Oakland's Mt. View Cemetery, three workers held signs protesting their treatment. No doubt they were struggling along at $1.1 million annually and were sympathetic to the plight of baseball players.

This was my second trip to Mt. View. I came here in April 1994, 14 hours after Mom told me she and Dad were divorcing. I felt uprooted and lost, insecure and desolate. Uncertain of what to do or where to go, I removed my dream from the shelf and drove 15 minutes to Ernie Lombardi's grave. The cemetery was serene and peaceful and still, qualities I craved.

Ernie's crypt was in an outside mausoleum. I remembered where it was and walked directly to it. He was on the fifth level, out of reach; I was sorry I couldn't touch it. This was the end, yet I did not rejoice. I laid on the ground and looked steadily at the sky. Five months after leaving amidst spring's rebirth, in both nature and baseball, it was now fall and the beginning of death. Everything had changed yet nothing had. Mom and Dad were living separate, happier lives and new people had entered my life with the magic of an afternoon breeze, though they were now far away. There was still life to face, and death, of course. There were struggles and joys and triumphs and tragedies.

Ernie Lombardi knew of struggling, and he looked it. The jowls and large nose and sad eyes gave him the face of a basset hound. But in his most famous picture, the face is not visible. Held together by tape and willpower, Ernie was knocked flat in a play at the plate and lay on the ground, helpless, in his infamous snooze as the great Dimaggio slid safely home. The game and World Series all but over, he picked himself up and resumed his spot behind the plate. He was back next year, hitting and catching like, well, like a Hall-of-Famer, and that is invincibility. Invincibility is in our perseverance, not our greatness. It is when we continue to walk and live and struggle amidst loss and pain, to know that life goes on and so must we, for there is always rebirth, there is always another season.

From my prone position, I was reverent. I sensed the bigness of things and my own littleness, but that's OK because I am but one of the thousands of blades of grass composing the unforgettable beauty of a ballpark, any ballpark. Though stepped on, divoted, cut or flooded, I will rise again, any who choose to do so will rise again, and that is the invincibility of summer.

About the Author

Dave D'Antonio grew up in Santa Clara, California, thinking and dreaming and playing baseball. He was a good-hitting shortstop who remembers his first base hit and still wonders how he missed making his Little League All-Star team. He graduated from the University of Redlands in 1982 with a double major in Political Science and Communications. A former journalist, D'Antonio now teaches American History and coaches wrestling at Bancroft Middle School. He lives in San Leandro, California, where he still thinks, dreams, and even plays baseball. This is his first book.